The Anti-Mary Exposed

THE ANTI-MARY EXPOSED

Rescuing the Culture From Toxic Femininity

Carrie Gress

TAN Books
Charlotte, North Carolina

Cover image: *The Immaculate Conception*, oil on canvas, (1767-1768), Giovannia Battista Tiepolo. Public domain via Wikimedia Commons. Image collage by Caroline Green.

Library of Congress Control Number: 2018966731

ISBN: 978-1-5051-1026-5

Published in the United States by
TAN Books
Charlotte, NC 28241
PO Box 410487
www.TANBooks.com

Printed in the United States of America

*For my sisters, who have taught me the true
and beautiful meaning of sisterhood*

Mary Boldy

Jill Faherty

Michelle Gress

Danielle Andrews

CONTENTS

INTRODUCTION

Women have been a mystery since Adam encountered Eve. But sometime over the last fifty years, a dark change has taken place in the lives of women and the men who love them. There is much confusion today about what it means to be a woman and even more confusion about how to treat them. The definitions of womanhood seem as numerous as there are people, with each woman trying to work out for herself who she is and how she ought to live her life. Meanwhile, men live in a constant state of shadowboxing, trying to stay in sync with the new progressive demands of womanhood.

Most of us, however, don't know the full story of the battle lines drawn in the 1960s that form the backdrop of what women think about themselves today. It is a story that is told by the victors—as most history is—where the events of the last fifty years unfolded as something chic, empowering, glamorous, important, and progressive. Or so goes the narrative. The reality, however, is something quite different. The clues, dropped like crumbs, can be seen along the way, though hastily covered up so that few can see the full underbelly of the movement.

One such crumb came from the early 1970s. Twelve (not an insignificant number) highly educated, upper class women sat around a table in New York City and chanted this "litany" to express what they wanted to see happen in the world:

"Why are we here today?" the chairwoman asked.

"To make revolution," they answered.

"What kind of revolution?" she replied.

"The Cultural Revolution," they chanted.

"And how do we make Cultural Revolution?" she demanded.

"By destroying the American family!" they answered.

"How do we destroy the family?" she came back.

"By destroying the American Patriarch," they cried exuberantly.

"And how do we destroy the American Patriarch?" she probed.

"By taking away his power!"

"How do we do that?"

"By destroying monogamy!" they shouted.

"How can we destroy monogamy?"

"By promoting promiscuity, eroticism, prostitution, abortion and homosexuality!" they resounded.[1]

These women had a very clear goal in mind and became the vanguard to what would become the women's liberation

---

[1]   Mallory Millett, "Marxist Feminism's Ruined Lives," *Front Page*, September 1, 2014, http://www.frontpagemag.com/fpm/240037/marxist-feminisms-ruined-lives-mallory-millett.

movement. Among them, perhaps, there were those who doubted they would succeed, but for those of us looking back, we know they succeeded. What they wanted—to promote "promiscuity, eroticism, prostitution, abortion and homosexuality"—has come to pass quite thoroughly in our culture today.

How is it, then, that the women's movement became such an unwieldy force that demolished so decisively the moral and social structures of American society? While many have suggested that it was "the sisterhood" that pulled radical feminists together, their grassroots effort cannot explain all of their success. The stories of the era tell of division and discord among second-wave feminist women and of heated debates over such things as *Cosmopolitan's* exploitation of women, lesbianism, and the politics of the group's leadership, which all threatened the project. That is, until they all found one topic to which they could hitch their wagons: *abortion*.

Sue Ellen Browder, author of *Subverted: How I Helped the Sexual Revolution Hijack the Women's Movement*[2] and former employee at *Cosmopolitan*, said that when she worked at the magazine, she regularly fabricated stories about fictional women known as the Cosmo Girl. "I could make her into anything I wanted her to be—a doctor, lawyer, judge, even a high-priced call girl—but there were two things she could not be if she was going to be glamorous, sophisticated, and cool: a virgin or a mother."[3]

2   Sue Ellen Browder, *Subverted: How I Helped the Sexual Revolution Hijack the Women's Movement* (San Francisco: Ignatius, 2015).
3   Sue Ellen Browder, phone conversation with author, August 14, 2018.

Second-wave feminism made it clear that children were the enemy, preventing women from fulfilling their dreams. Thus, abortion became a necessity and was legalized in 1973 as the Vietnam War was coming to an end. Fatalities of that war—58,220 US servicemen total—were quickly dwarfed by this new kind of killing, mothers killing their own children (sixty million and counting; three thousand daily in the US alone). Today, abortion is by far the leading cause of death in the United States annually, significantly outpacing heart disease and cancer. It kills more than the equivalent of total US fatalities in Vietnam every three weeks.

What happens, then, when you have generations of people that have willfully killed their own children through abortion? The medievals were against abortion because it takes an innocent life, but also because they knew it was mortally damaging to the human soul of those who engaged in it. It isn't just a child that dies in an abortion, but something in the mother and the father and the whole family that dies as well.

As St. Thomas Aquinas said, *bonum est diffusivum sui*, the good spreads itself out. Similarly, evil spreads itself out. The grave evil of abortion has reached into every area of familial life and left society morally threadbare. Our news feed confirms this daily with headlines like "Abortion Activists Kill Baby Jesus in Graphic Abortion on Virgin Mary Outside Catholic Church,"[4] "Colorado Woman Killed Newborn

---

4   Steven Ertelt, "Abortion Activist Kill Baby Jesus in Graphic Abortion on Virgin Mary Outside Catholic Church," *Life News*, March 15, 2013, https://www.lifenews.com/2017/03/15/abortion-activists-kill-baby-jesus-in-graphic-abortion-on-virgin-mary-outside-catholic-church/.

Baby and Tossed It on Neighbor's Deck,"[5] or *Teen Vogue's* "Anal Sex: What You Need to Know." The layers of confusion, twisted thinking, decadence, sacrilege, and viciousness descend ever-deeper with each passing day. Rage, obscenity, sexual license, nudity, erasing of gender differences, and the cheapening of life have all become commonplace in the public square. Women haven't just listed a bit to the wayward side of the moral compass; they shattered the compass. Almost overnight, our once pro-life culture became pro-lifestyle, returning to an epicurean paganism that embraces everything that feels good. Like a wildfire blowing through dry tinder, these dramatic changes burned through the lives of millions and millions of women, men, and children, with little to nothing to stop it.

Outside Influence

The scale and scope of the evil we see in our culture begs us to ask: could there be something behind this? Are there outside pressures, "like a roaring lion, seeking some one to devour" (1 Pt 5:8), that have been influencing humanity, particularly women, over the last five decades? Paul Kengor, in his book *Takedown: From Communists to Progressives, How the Left has Sabotaged Family and Marriage*, lays out the political and intellectual pieces that have led to the destruction of the family. He concludes at one point, however, when talking about the influence communists and progressives have had

---

5   Katherine Lam, "Colorado Woman Killed Newborn Baby and Tossed It on Neighbor's Deck," *Fox News,* March 21, 2018, https://www.foxnews.com/us/colorado-woman-killed-newborn-baby-and-tossed-it-on-neighbors-deck-police-say.

upon young people through universities, that there has to be more to the story than just rhetoric. "Why do people in our universities fall so easily for this vapid claptrap so contrary to their human nature?" he asks. "Their impressionable youth alone is not a sufficient explanation."[6] Kengor makes clear that the pieces just don't add up to the sum of their parts—there must be more to it.

Bishop Robert Barron concludes something similar about the violence and dramatic loss of life in the twentieth century—the bloodiest century ever. The auxiliary bishop of the Archdiocese of Los Angeles says:

> Look at the twentieth century, bloodiest on record, no question about that. The number of people killed for ideological purposes and warfare was the worst ever. Can you explain that entirely on psychological or political categories? It just seems comically inadequate to the reality. To say that Hitler, Stalin, Mao, et cetera. . . . are simply explicable politically or psychologically? I don't know. There is something about the pervasiveness of violence and the destruction of life in the twentieth century that has all the marks of the Murderer from the beginning.[7]

---

6   Paul Kengor, *Takedown: From Communists to Progressives, How the Left has Sabotaged Family and Marriage* (Washington, DC:WND Books, 2016), 138.

7   Robert Barron, "Reflections on the Devil," *Word on Fire*, video, July 25, 2012, https://www.wordonfire.org/resources/video/reflections-on-the-devil/248/.

Something beyond human vice, Bishop Barron concludes, must be behind the bloodshed of the twentieth century. The marks of the devil are all there: bloodshed, extinguishing of life, disunity, and confusion.

Upon reflection, seeing the demonic source behind the geopolitical death and destruction of the last century is relatively easy. But is there, similarly, a uniquely malevolent source promoting abortion and the new behavior that women have fallen into, wittingly or not? Just asking the question in this context almost forces the conclusion that there must be something more than simple human vice behind the fact that millions of women have betrayed the most sacred and fundamental of relationships, that of mother and child. The first two parts of this book provide the evidence and argument supporting that conclusion and reveal the hidden identity and manifestations of this insatiable anti-Marian spirit targeting women today.

The changes that we have seen over the last half-century go well beyond effective teaching, psychology, politics, and fancy marketing. Yes, all of these have played a role in influencing our culture, but there is most certainly another actor involved in the deconstruction of the family. Yes, like Bishop Barron sees in the twentieth century, the marks of extinguishing life, disunity, and confusion are there, but there is something new that seems to be pointed directly at the heart and soul of women. The attack has been directed at the very areas where women are able to reflect the love, goodness, and likeness of the Virgin Mary: in their virginity and motherhood.

In addition to the direct attack on the Virgin Mother and those who follow her model of womanhood, there has also been a significant rise in the occult and pagan goddess worship among women. Basic witchcraft items can now be purchased at places like Sephora and Target, and tarot card reading, astrologers, and psychics are common in our cities and smaller towns. National calls to put hexes upon politicians are no longer unusual, nor is children's entertainment that engages in the subtler nuances of witchcraft. Even the 2018 Thanksgiving issue of the *Washington Post Magazine* prominently featured witchcraft and satanic rituals as normal avenues for those seeking meaning in life.[8]

In the wake of these cultural trends lie the powerful and heart-wrenching realities of those attached to women under the anti-Marian spell: husbands wondering what happened to their wives who have left them for a different life (or another woman), fathers wondering what has happened to their daughters, and children wondering what has happened to their mothers.

To say that there is ample evidence for the argument contained in this book would be an understatement. Two years of research have provided story after story of the terrible things women are doing to themselves and to their husbands, children, and grandchildren: stories like the woman who stabbed her twenty-month-old granddaughter and then baked her in the oven, the protestors wearing t-shirts that say "Men Are Trash," the baby gender reveal party that served

---

8   Kate Warren, "Spellbound," *Washington Post Magazine,* November 18, 2018, 32–39.

red jelly-filled donuts to announce the parents' decision to abort, pastors blessing abortion clinics, or Cate Blanchet's announcement that her vagina is her moral compass. The examples are legion. We have largely grown numb to them, assuming that this is just abnormal behavior from women on the fringes of society. And yet these are not all done by the crazy, psychotic, or forgotten underbelly. These kinds of atrocities are often taking place and encouraged in some form in our homes, schools, hospitals, and even churches by normal and everyday women.

This book, although it engages in the heavy battles at hand, will not end with the anti-Mary having the last word. Gratefully, we have the real Mary who is present in the world, in our lives, and who is capable of the miraculous. With an unparalleled track record, our spiritual mother is far from distant, superficial, or saccharine. She is the true model of authentic femininity and offers us her assistance through all of life's demands, struggles, frustrations, and tears. She brings clarity, healing, peace, joy, and grace wherever she is invited. She offers us the key to unlock the confusion about what it means to be women and what we need to do to find the true happiness that our souls crave.

PART I

The Long Battle

CHAPTER I

Erasing Mary

"I will place enmity between you and the woman."

—Genesis 3:15

"We are now standing in the face of the great-est historical confrontation humanity has gone through," said the archbishop of Krakow, Karol Wojtyla, in 1978. "I do not think that wide circles of American society or wide circles of the Christian community realize this fully." The future pope continued somberly, "We are now facing the final confrontation between the Church and the anti-Church, of the Gospel versus the anti-Gospel."[1]

Archbishop Wojtyla, by comparing the Church to an anti-Church and the Gospel to the anti-Gospel, was pick-ing up on the ancient thread of Christ and the antichrist. Pulling on the thread of Genesis 3:15, the archbishop could

---

[1]   Karol Wojtyla, "Bicentennial talk given in the United States," in C. John McCloskey, "The Final Confrontation," *The Catholic Thing*, June 1, 2014, https://www.thecatholicthing.org/2014/06/01/the-final-confrontation/.

3

have easily added to this list a confrontation between Mary and the anti-Mary. But just what would this be, and would it be related to Our Lady and culture today? The answer is intimately tied up with who Mary of Nazareth is.

Antichrist and Anti-Mary

The antichrist is an idea that dates back to the earliest Church. Most people associate it with a single person who is supposed to come at the end of the age. This specific antichrist is mentioned in several places in Scripture, by name or more generically, but particularly in St. John's letters and St. Paul's letter to the Thessalonians (see 1 Jn 2:18; 2 Thes 8–11).

St. John, writing in the first century, says, "Every spirit that does not confess Jesus is not of God. This is the spirit of antichrist, of which you heard that it was coming, and now it is in the world already" (1 Jn 4:3). Here, the apostle Jesus loved speaks of the antichrist as both an actual individual and also a general spirit. Elsewhere, St. John repeats his warning against a spirit contrary to Jesus: "Many deceivers have gone out into the world, men who will not acknowledge the coming of Jesus Christ in the flesh; such a one is the deceiver and the antichrist" (2 Jn 1:7).

St. Paul, although he doesn't use the word *antichrist*, also speaks of a spirit opposed to Christ. He warns those in the early Church, "I am afraid that as the serpent deceived Eve by his cunning, your thoughts will be led astray from a sincere and pure devotion to Christ. For if someone comes and preaches another Jesus than the one we preached, or if you receive a different spirit from the one you received, or if you accept a different gospel from the one you accepted, you submit to it readily enough" (2 Cor 11:3–4). St. Paul, knowing how easy it is to fall into sin, warns against accepting this spirit opposed to Christ.

Because of the familiarity Christians have with a notion of an antichrist, it isn't a stretch to comprehend an anti-Church or an anti-Gospel. Even the term anti-apostle was adopted by the Soviet Communists for their secret infiltration of agents into seminaries to corrupt the Church from the inside out.[2] Adding the idea of an "anti-Mary" to this list makes sense for several reasons.

First, we know that Our Lady brings a unique spirit into the world as the Mother of God. She is the anti-Eve. Her yes reversed the curse that Adam and Eve brought to humanity through Original Sin. Mary's *fiat* reverses Eve's rejection of God and his will for humanity. "As a woman brought humanity under the power of Satan," one theologian, echoing early Church Father St. Irenaeus, explained, "God would liberate humanity with the cooperation of a woman."[3]

---

[2]   Marie Carre, *AA-1025: Memoirs of the Communist Infiltration into the Church* (Charlotte: TAN Books, 2009).

[3]   Francesco Bamonte, *The Virgin Mary and the Devil in Exorcisms* (Paoline, 2014), 37. Here Fr. Bamonte is following the great St. Irenaeus, who wrote, "As the human race was subjected to death through [the act of] a virgin, so was it saved by a virgin, and thus the disobedience of one virgin was precisely balanced by the obedience of another." St. Irenaeus, "Against Heresies," ed. Cyril Richardson, *Early Christian Fathers* (New York: Collier Books, 1970), Book V, 19.

Second, the potential of an anti-Mary is related to Mary's status as the New Eve. If Christ is the New Adam and Mary the New Eve, it makes sense to consider that an antichrist could have a female complement.[4] Yes, there is potential that this anti-Mary could be a specific individual, but there is also the possibility for there to be *an anti-Marian spirit that animates an entire movement and the individuals engaged in it.*

Another significant reason for suggesting that an anti-Marian spirit has gripped our culture is because of the overwhelming evidence that women are suffering the punishment St. Paul foretold to the Thessalonians. St. Paul describes a lawless one who will come and deceive many because "they refused to love the truth and so be saved. Therefore God send upon them a strong delusion, to make them believe what is false" (2 Thes 2:9–12). In essence, what St. Paul is warning against are those who come to deceive others. People not attached to the truth of Christ will live with strong delusions, believing what is false. This is precisely the kind of delusion that has bewitched so many contemporary women to willingly fall in line with the anti-Marian spirit of our age. The abortion numbers are telling: never in history have mothers been so willing to kill their own children. As St. Paul warned, it is fair to say that some "cunning serpent" has made its way into the hearts of women and led them very far astray.

---

4   There are several uses of the term "antimary" published online prior to my own independent use of the word.

The Longest Battle

There is yet another reason to consider a high-pitched conflict between Mary and an anti-Mary: the battle between "the Woman" in Scripture and the serpent. The standoff between Satan and Mary straddles Scripture like bookends; the primordial struggle between them started in Genesis and ends in Revelation.

In Genesis, after the fall of Eve, we read, "I will put enmities between thee and the woman, and thy seed and her seed: she shall crush thy head, and thou shalt lie in wait for her heel" (Gen. 3:15 DV). Here God is speaking to the serpent, Satan, to declare the chasm that exists between those that follow "the woman" and those who follow him.

This enmity returns at the end of Scripture, in Revelation:

> A great sign appeared in heaven, a woman clothed with the sun, with the moon under her feet, and on her head a crown of twelve stars; she was with child and she cried out in her pangs of birth, in anguish for delivery. And another sign appeared in heaven; behold, a great red dragon. . . . And the dragon stood before the woman who was about to bear a child, that he might devour her child when she brought it forth; she brought forth a male child, one who is to rule all the nations with a rod of iron, but her child was caught up to God and to his throne (Rv 12:1–5).

When Scripture speaks of Satan's demise in this confrontation, it does so in a Marian context. Pope St. John II noted in his encyclical *Redemptoris Mater* that Mary is "located in the center itself of the enmity."[5] Of course, Mary's Son is the principal victor, but he does so, explicitly, as *her* Son. So important is this mother/son relationship that St. Irenaeus concludes, "The enemy would not have been justly conquered unless it had been a man [made] of a woman who conquered him."[6]

Mary's centrality in the battle between God and Satan gives her a unique status among the saints. Dante spoke of her special role to disperse God's graces to humanity in his *Divine Comedy*: "We venerate Mary with all the impetus of our hearts, of our affections, of our desires. That is how he wants it, he who established that we receive everything by means of Mary." Dante's faith in Mary's role is confirmed by the saints. St. Jacinta, one of the seers of Our Lady at Fatima, told her cousin Lucia, "Tell everyone that God concedes his graces by means of the Immaculate Heart of Mary. They should ask for them from her."[7] And St. John Paul affirms that, while she has a subordinate role to Christ, Mary's mediation "shares in the one unique source that is the mediation of Christ himself." He continues:

> This role is at the same time special and extraordinary. It flows from her divine motherhood and can be understood and lived in faith only on the basis of the full truth of this motherhood. Since by virtue of divine election Mary is the earthly Mother of the Father's consubstantial Son and his "generous companion" in the work of

5   Pope St. John Paul II, *Redemptoris Mater,* March 25, 1987, no. 11.
6   St. Irenaeus, "Against Heresies," Book V, 31.
7   Bramonte, *Virgin Mary and Exorcisms*, 99.

redemption "she is a mother to us in the order of grace." This role constitutes a real dimension of her presence in the saving mystery of Christ and the Church.[8]

Mary's place in the order of grace also elevates her significance in direct battle with demons. When commanded by priests during exorcisms, demons testify to the rage they feel toward Mary, a mere human with such an exalted position. As an exorcist attests, "The cooperation of Mary in the victory of God over the demons humiliates them more than if God defeated them alone. To be defeated by God through a cooperation of a human creature, inferior by nature yet Immaculate, greatly humiliates their bloated pride."[9] For this reason, during exorcisms, "demons are often angrier and more furious in Mary's regard than that of God himself."[10]

The great battle between Mary and the devil plays out daily on our screens and the pages of magazines, in our marriages and bedrooms, in abortion clinics and doctors' offices, on sports fields, in schools and shopping malls, and everywhere else women have to make choices about how they will live their lives and care (or not care) for those around them. The lines couldn't be starker. But like Eve before them, so many women have unwittingly fallen into the dragon's trap. Simply treading water with the rest of the culture and the social cues from the media elite, more often than not, most women have never stopped to consider the full implications of their decisions: the eternal ramifications

---

[8]   John Paul II, *Redemptoris Mater*, no. 38
[9]   Bramonte, *Virgin Mary and Exorcisms*, 37.
[10]   Bramonte, *Virgin Mary and Exorcisms*, 37.

of aborting a child, contracepting, or nurturing narcissism in their own souls.

The Anti-Marian Appearance

If there is, indeed, an anti-Marian spirit, what might it look like? Well, a woman in its grip would not value children. She would be bawdy, vulgar, and angry. She would rage against the idea of anything resembling humble obedience or self-sacrifice for others. She would be petulant, shallow, catty, and overly sensuous. She would also be self-absorbed, manipulative, gossipy, anxious, and self-servingly ambitious. In short, she would be everything that Mary is not. She would bristle especially at the idea of being a virgin or a mother.

Women have always desired equality and respect, but our current culture isn't seeking it through the grace of Mary; rather, the culture seeks this equality and respect through the vices of Machiavelli: rage, intimidation, tantrums, bullying, raw emotion, and absence of logic. It is this aggressive impulse—this toxic femininity—that finds pride in calling oneself "nasty," feels empowered by dressing as a vagina, belittles men, and sees the (tragically ironic) need to drop civility so that civility can somehow return again.

The devil knows that all these marks of the anti-Mary— rage, indignation, vulgarity, and pride—short-circuit a woman's greatest gifts: wisdom, prudence, patience, unflappable peace, intuition, her ability to weave together the fabric of society, and her capacity for a deep and fulfilling relationship with God. Instead, the father of lies promises power, fame, fortune, and sterile, fleeting pleasures.

A striking clue that all these things we witness in abundance today are at odds with God's plan for women is that, for all the so-called progress women have made, there is precious little evidence that any of it has actually made women happier. Divorce rates are still staggering, with 70 percent initiated by women; suicide rates are soaring; drug and alcohol abuse is unprecedented; STDs, particularly among women, are at epidemic levels, and depression and anxiety are everywhere. Women are not getting happier, just more medicated.

Another clue that all these claims to simple undifferentiated equality are fictitious arises in times of crisis. In disasters, such as hurricanes or mass shootings, it is predominantly men who man the boats to rescue those in need or offer their bodies to protect women from the spray of bullets. In dire situations, for all the talk of equality, the heroic nature of men cannot be suppressed. Women certainly can be, and often are, but their true heroism is usually expressed in ways more in keeping with their nature: in imitating Mary rather than men.

No Moms, No Mary

The treatment of motherhood over the last fifty years is one of the first signs that we are dealing with a radically new movement. Mothers (both spiritual and biological) are a natural icon of Mary. A mother helps others know who Mary is by her generosity, kindness, patience, compassion, peace, intuition, and ability to nurture souls. Mary's love (and the love of mothers) offers one of the best images of what God's love is like—unconditional, healing, safe, and deeply personal.

The last few decades have witnessed the subtle erasing of the Marian icon in real women. First, through the pill, followed by the advent of legalized abortion, motherhood has been on the chopping block along with childhood. Motherhood has become dispensable to the point that today the broader culture doesn't bat an eye when a child is adopted by two men.

Every culture until ours has known how critical a mother is (even in her imperfection) to nurture a child to healthy adulthood and spiritual maturity. No culture can renew itself without spiritual maturity. Yes, there are many people who have lost their mothers for one reason or another, but most would agree that, truly, there are few things as tragic. Such sad realities only strengthen the argument that children need mothers rather than diminish their importance.

In the '60s, Betty Friedan argued that mothers were over-nurturing their children and that heading to work would prevent us from smothering them. Germaine Greer said that childbearing "was never intended to be as time-consuming and self-conscious a process as it is. One of the deepest evils in our society is tyrannical nurturance."[11] These women might be happy to know that we now spend 50 percent less time with our children than we did five

---

[11]   This quote and several others from Gloria Steinem, Germaine Greer, and other radical feminists are sourced from several different places online.

decades ago. Yet the late, great Kate O'Beirne reports, "By every available measure, including school achievement and the incidence of delinquency, depression, sexual promiscuity, suicide, and substance abuse, the well-being of American children has declined in recent decades."[12] It can be no accident that we are witnessing unprecedented emotional and mental trauma and brokenness in every segment of our population because motherhood has been so devalued and neglected. As economist James Tooley described it, "We've swapped a society where women could be full-time mothers—a role many found fulfilling and satisfying—for one that fuels consumerism and clogs our roads with second cars on the drive to school, where spoiled children, buried under mountains of toys they can't be bothered to play with, watch suggestive TV shows in their lonely bedrooms. And we have this partly because the equality feminists force us to believe that motherhood was parasitic, the housewife a leech."[13]

The move to make mothers into leeches and unleash our children from over-nurturing has, like many of the presumptuous platitudes of radical feminism, turned out to be entirely wrong.

Dignity's Source

If one were to ask where the radical notion that women are equal to men came from, where do you suppose we would find our answer? It didn't come from the Greeks: Aristotle

---

12   Kate O'Beirne, *Women Who Make the World Worse* (New York: Sentinel, 2006), xxii.
13   James Tooley, *The Miseducation of Women* (Chicago: Ivan R, 2003), 192.

and others called us "deformed males." It didn't come from
Judaism: though given some status, a broad movement to
promote the dignity of woman never materialized, and the
practice of polygamy remained. Asian religions, such as Bud-
dhism or Hinduism, didn't start it. And it certainly hasn't
come from Islam.

Nineteenth-century scholar William Lecky (a non-
Catholic) gives us the answer: "No longer the slave or toy
of man, no longer associated only with ideas of degradation
and of sensuality, woman rose, in the person of the Virgin
Mother, into a new sphere, and became the object of rever-
ential homage, of which antiquity has no conception. . . .
A new type of character was called into being; a new kind
of admiration was fostered. Into a harsh and ignorant and
benighted age, this ideal type infused a conception of gentleness and purity, unknown to the proudest civilizations of
the past."[14]

Sadly, few in our culture know that they owe a debt of
gratitude to Catholicism for the notion that women are equal
to men. Throughout the gospels, Christ treated women with
dignity, and over the centuries veneration of the Virgin Mary
further developed the notion that women are equal to men.

It might seem that equality among men and women is
obvious, a simple intuition any thinking person would have.
But if so, why didn't any other religious movement see it?
Because it was Mary who turned the sins of Eve upside down
and allowed this now-commonplace notion to take root.

---

[14]   William Lecky, *History of Rationalism*, vol. 1 (Longmans, Green,
and Co., 1866), 234–35.

Christianity, though largely abandoned by secular culture, remains the source for this profound insight.

The anti-Mary, then, is a sophisticated and aloof sort of slavery, where nothing is too evil or too bad to try, but also where every effort is made to erase the naturally imprinted icon of Our Lady stamped into the body and soul of every woman. More than anything, however, the anti-Marian woman does not know that she is loved passionately and deeply by a heavenly Father, a Father who wants nothing more than to meet the deepest desires of her heart and who delights in her as his child, his creation, his unique and unrepeatable daughter.

Culture and society started with women and followed her cues. The hands that rocked the cradle formed the future. Even in the days of foraging, women, because of their physical needs and the needs of children, remained at the hearth, where men would return with food to supply their tribes. But this spark of civilization didn't stop there; it continued to evolve into more and more sophisticated versions. Archbishop Fulton Sheen speaks of the role women play in the ascent of culture: "Culture derives from woman—for had she not taught her children to talk, the great spiritual values of the world would not have passed from generation to generation. After nourishing the substance of the body to which she gave birth, she then nourishes the child with the substance of her mind. As guardian of the values of the spirit, as protectress of the mortality of the young, she preserves culture, which deals with purposes and ends, while man upholds civilization, which deals only with means."[15]

Culture ascended to new levels with the arrival of Our Lady. Slowly but steadily, Catholic culture became saturated with the idea of Mary as the model for Christian womanhood. She also became the inspiration for Christian manhood across Europe. Art historian Sir Kenneth Clark remarked that Mary "taught a race of tough and ruthless barbarians the virtues of tenderness and compassion."[16]

"If we were to lose Mary," Pope Pius X explained, "the world would wholly decay. Virtue would disappear, especially holy purity and virginity, connubial love and fidelity. The mystical river through which God's graces flow to us would dry up. The brightest star would disappear from heaven, and darkness would take its place."[17] While it may have been difficult to image this at the time of the pope's writing in the early twentieth century, it isn't any longer. Indeed, most evidence indicates clearly that we are living in this darkness.

---

[15]   Fulton J. Sheen, *The World's First Love*, 2nd Edition (San Francisco: Ignatius Press, 2010), 188–89.

[16]   Kenneth Clark, *Civilization*, DVD series, BBC Production, 2006.

[17]   Quoted in Josef Cardinal Mindszenty, *The Face of the Heavenly Mother* (New York: Philosophical Library, 1951), 83.

Chapter 2

Satan's Point of Entry: The Malcontent Heart

"Envy is thin because it bites but never eats."

—Spanish Proverb

Stories are one of the earliest teaching tools known to man. Tales and epic adventures told around fires passed along lessons to teach the next generation about life and about what it means to be a man, a woman, a family, a tribe.

One of the best-known stories of all ages goes back to Eve. We know it well. She is tempted by Satan to eat of the fruit of the tree from which God told her not to eat. When she hesitated, Satan dangled the bait: "You will not die. For God knows that when you eat of it your eyes will be opened, and you will be like God, knowing good and evil" (Gn 3:4–5). He knew how to get to her—to offer her something appealing that she didn't already have. This ancient story tells us something about the deep vices of women.

Men and women living together in a state of grace are an icon of God, made in his image and likeness, building each other up. But the opposite is also true. The man and woman outside the state of grace can quickly become an icon of Satan—portraying his vices, particularly envy and pride—while also mutually tearing each other apart. A quick look at Harvey Weinstein and the parade of women who either auditioned or who helped facilitate the auditioning on his "casting couch" is revealing. Their mutual collaboration, when it was mutual, was denigrating, not edifying. And when it wasn't mutual, it was devastating.

It's easy to find trenchant criticism of men and their faults (and of course, they are abundant in our age), but there is very little available content that considers the vices and weaknesses of women. Feminism has made such conversations impossible. If a man engages in pointing out a woman's faults, he is sexist; if a woman does, she is ignorant or blaming the victim (because all women are victims, as we will see later). But it doesn't serve women well to ignore our faults and failings.

Deep in the heart of most women is the desire to want more. This desire, like most things, can be directed to the good, as in wanting more of God's will, or it can be directed to the bad, such as wanting more of something no matter what the cost. Sociologist Joyce Benenson, who has seen this phenomenon among women the world over, offers an explanation.[1] The reality is that motherhood is hardwired

---

[1]   Joyce Benenson and Henry Markovits, *Warriors and Worriers* (Oxford University Press, 2014).

into a woman's soul, whether she is conscious of it or not. The motherhood dimension of women plays itself out in many ways, but particularly in two: 1) women are weaker than men, so they can't go about getting things based purely on physical strength; and 2) when women are pregnant and having children, they are in a very vulnerable position because they are not able to go hunt for food, or get a job with ease to keep all the mouths fed and bodies clothed. In other words, women have fundamental vulnerabilities for which they must find ways to compensate. The natural solution throughout most of history was to look for a husband to take care of the necessities. This is simply the way that families are built, sustained, and future generations are brought into the world. But every woman, with or without a husband, still faces a world of uncertainty. Fear, lack of control, hunger, and loss of status are all motivating factors for a woman to want more, to protect herself and her children.

Problems arise, however, when women use their vices, rather than their virtues, to get what they want or need. Because there are a limited number of good husbands to be gotten, or opportunities are scarce, women who find themselves competing against other women often resort to destructive ways to edge out the others. Virginia Woolf captured the vicious element of female competition in her essay "Room of One's Own":

> A woman dresses "to kill," to arouse
> Jealous, devastate other women, to "star" in
> The room, to make an economic/romantic
> "killing" with a man. Some women take the

> beauty of other women as a personal
> Affront; their first cool, side-glance
> Appraisal dissolves into a little girl's pout.
> This fear of a gain in women, so often
> Criticized as proof of her narcissism, is not
> That. She is desperately trying to outlive her
> Approved shelf life.
> Women will stop being dependent and
> Masochistic when they are free. For now,
> Women are just as bad as men in the matter
> Of their slavery, to which they cling.[2]

The stakes for women are high, and what women fear are not trifles. Women throughout history have experienced real and genuine hardships, struggles, and pain associated with the weaknesses of our human state. Women often carry burdens of fear or hurt to which they respond to with a desire to control situations or others. Others try to avoid vulnerability and steel themselves against anything that could hurt them again. These are the types of scenarios that have led to so many jaded, cynical, and defensive women.

The curious piece of this puzzle, however, is the way in which women compete for limited resources. The competition cannot be an open one. Women won't tolerate, Benenson says, other women who are openly competing with them, so the competition happens quietly and subtly. "Women honestly believe they are not competing and will

---

2   Quoted in Phyllis Chesler, *A Politically Incorrect Feminist* (St. Martin's Press, 2018), loc. 432, Kindle.

not tolerate a woman they think is competing."[3] The desire to conceal open competition is innate in women, starting at the tenderest of ages in young girls. When the competition surfaces somehow, making things tense, women defuse it by automatically smiling intensely to present a veneer of kindness in the face of conflict. When hidden conflict becomes open conflict, it usually does not amount to punches thrown, as so often happens with the other sex, but behind the scenes with backstabbing and manipulation.

Competition is not the only thing to be avoided; so is non-conformity. Women operate on a fundamentally egalitarian model. "One girl cannot be seen to be superior to another," Benenson says, "not in plain sight at least."[4] These situations play themselves out every day in the workplace, with a significant proportion of women preferring not to work under another woman. A large percentage of women, Benenson reports, will not help a female subordinate unless there is some sort of *quid pro quo*, perhaps fearing that her own position would be threatened by a rising colleague. This egalitarian model is very different from the hierarchical model evidenced among men. Rather than seeing others, particularly subordinates, as competition, men have a more fundamental capacity to see how those with different gifts can be useful for the common good since, unlike women, they don't live with this sense of vulnerability. This is not to say women don't have this capacity to see the good in

---

3   Benenson, *Warriors and Worriers,* 177.

4   Ibid., 181.

others—they do—but this is a virtue they must more consciously develop.

The most toxic situations for female relationships, resulting in the frequent, albeit hidden, violence, is a polygamous family where "sister-wives" are constantly competing for resources, for themselves and their children. Open conflict in such situations usually does not erupt, but quiet and hidden sabotage of other women's property or children is a common form of aggression. Though polygamy is illegal and rare, it is not far from the dynamic in which many women, working for a single boss, compete for attention and limited promotions. Perhaps this is why women often don't treat each other well in the workplace.

The innate strain for resources takes its toll on a woman's thought patterns, character, and sense of happiness. Many women desire more than what they currently have or are. The common complaint of many women reflects some kind of discontent best summarized as the desire "to have it all." The "I want it all!" mentality has stirred endless national debates for decades, fed by rhetoric such as Gloria Steinem's cool assurance, "You are woman. You can do everything a man can do and do it better. You can have it all." Women continue in their quest to find the perfect job, husband, home, children, travel schedule, leisure time, and enough me time to achieve personal fulfillment. Magazines and media, as we shall see later, often serve as bellows fanning the flames of a woman's malcontent by subtly hinting that she is a victim, that there is more out there that she is missing, or perhaps that she chose the wrong mate, career, or lifestyle. All these types of subtle signals have the collective effect of destabilizing a woman, leaving her guessing about what more she ought to have or be doing rather than resting in gratitude for what she may already have.

The answer, of course, is that no woman can have all of this, but this illusion doesn't curb the female desire for it. Betty Friedan, in *The Feminine Mystique*, touched upon this longing in the woman's heart of the 1960s when she asked, "Is this all?" She described it as "the ache without a name." But the ache she described was not unique to the women of the 1960s; it is a universal restlessness that cannot be resolved until the heart rests in God. Since Friedan asked the question six decades ago, women have tried every ill-conceived thing under the sun to fill this heart hole, the *Capax Dei,* that we all have, that only God can fill. But without this Divine Key that fits perfectly in the feminine heart, Satan has a point of entry: our discontent. "If only I had *x*, or if only I could do *y*," the running dialogue goes in our heads, "then I would be happy." But wisdom and experience tell us that even when we get *x* or *y*, we find yet another *x* to yearn for shortly thereafter, which comes, yet again, with the false promise of authentic satisfaction.

This discontent acts as a seed in our soul that, if we feed with jealousy, envy, cunning, gossip, and conniving, only pushes us further away from the one thing that can bring satisfaction. But oh, how women have been encouraged to nurture it! History is full of stories of a woman feeding what started as a prick of discontent that grew into her own destruction. It is exactly this seed of discontent that opens women to the anti-Marian spirit, the perfect nourishment for its malignant fruit.

The Modern Fairy Tale

If we look back again to the idea of stories, particularly fairy tales, there is ample evidence of many a woman's ruin because of malcontent. *Snow White, Cinderella, The Little Mermaid, Rapunzel, Sleeping Beauty*—these are the stories that have animated the imaginations of little girls for centuries. Popularized by Disney, different versions of these stories, particularly *Cinderella*, have crossed the divides of cultures and time throughout much of history. Fairy tales help us understand that we can and should overcome adversity. They tell us a great deal about the static nature of humanity. Were human nature ever-shifting, as our culture would have us believe, they would not continue to resonate with us the way they have for millennia.

Fairy tales such as these often follow a particular story pattern. There is generally an older woman—a mother, witch, or queen—who relishes her position as top cat, and then some upstart comes along and threatens her prized place as "fairest of them all." The young maiden must, at all costs, be stopped. And from there, the fairy tales unfold into a common ending: things don't go well for the old hag and the young maiden and her prince live happily ever after.

There are many lessons that can be extracted from such fairy tales, but often a primary issue is the timeless vice of envy, offering a keen window into a discontented heart. Envy and jealousy are generally used interchangeably, but they are actually quite distinct. Jealousy is a desire directed at a particular good or object, but the desire stops there. Envy takes jealousy to a new level—it wants something, but it sees the person who has the desired object, or who is an obstacle to it, to be taking something away from them. The word *envy* comes from the Latin word *invidere*, which means to "look askance upon," or to give someone an "evil eye" full of malice and spite. Envy fosters the impulse to destroy others and, unlike over vices, does not have pleasure as its end; unlike gluttony or lust, there is nothing pleasurable about being envious. It has been insightfully described as "a vice few can avoid yet nobody craves, for to experience envy is to feel small and inferior, a loser shrink-wrapped in spite."[5] Such are the old women in our fairy tales.

Because envy is such a commonplace vice, it isn't surprising to see the role it plays in radical feminism, but what is most curious is to see the similarities between it and the pattern of fairy tales whose plots are dripping with vice. Envy's first and foremost role plays out in the relationship radical feminists have come to have with their children. The ideology behind unfettered abortion, we are told, is that it must exist so that women can get ahead. A child's life is a threat— *the* threat—to the mother's success and happiness. Much like *Snow White*, the child is silenced, but for much longer than one hundred years. How else is it that people could come to rejoice in such an act of destruction, or think it empowering to "shout your abortion," or to tell others about your favorite abortion, like Martha Plimpton recently has.

And what about men? Men usually don't figure into fairy tales as antagonists, but our contemporary version has set

---

5   Natalie Angier, "In Pain and Joy of Envy the Brain May Play a Role," *The New York Times*, February 16, 2009, https://www.ny-times.com/2009/02/17/science/17angi.html.

its sights on them. Women decided that if only they could have the lives that men had, then they would be happy. The attitude they often take toward men reveals the destructive and belittling marks of envy. Women no longer embrace the goodness that men have to offer society but view it as an evil that must be eliminated. The important impulses of protection and responsibility that have so often inspired men to greatness have been reduced to "toxic masculinity." The unspoken feminist mantra says, "Men, even though we want to be just like you, you must change." The venom of envy is directed daily at men, particularly on the ubiquitous TV ads and shows where every one of them bumbles along until a sage woman comes to the rescue.

And how do feminist women treat those women who don't embrace their ideals? Women who choose to have many children or pick family over career are frequently disparaged as fools and, on occasion, are compared to rabbits. (Many feminists seem to miss the irony that "sexually liberated women" literally dress up like rabbits—or bunnies—to show their empowerment.) Arizona senator Krysten Sinema made it clear what she thinks about stay-at-home moms: "These women who act like staying at home, leeching off their husbands or boyfriends, and just cashing the checks, is some sort of feminism because they're choosing to live that life. . . . That's bulls***. I mean, what the f*** are we really talking about here?"[6] Speaking of motherhood, Supreme

---

6   Hank Berrien, "Krysten Simena, Stay-at-Home-Moms 'Leech Off their Husbands,'" *Daily Wire*, October 19, 2018, https://www. dailywire.com/news/37369/kyrsten-sinema-stay-home-moms-leech-their-husbands-hank-berrien.

Court justice Ruth Bader Ginsburg said, "Motherly love ain't everything it has been cracked up to be. To some extent it's a myth that men have created to make women think that they do this job to perfection." One sociologist in the '70s went so far as to suggest that "to be happy in a relationship which imposes so many impediments on her, as traditional marriage does, women must be slightly mentally ill."[7]

Over and over, the importance of the "sisterhood" is extolled, with Madeleine Albright chiming in that "there is a special place in Hell for women who don't help other women." But the sisterhood is extended only to those women who check off the right ideological boxes. Support for abortion is an imperative, otherwise the sisterhood not only neglects a particular woman, it seeks to destroy her politically. The treatment received by Sarah Palin and Sarah Huckabee at the hands of radical feminists is a sample of how the rules of the sisterhood change when the politics of abortion come into play.

One of the more telling trends of our day is the continual fixation even liberated women have with royalty and the ideal of being a princess. Despite their allegiance to aloof sophistication and radical independence, magazines such as *Cosmopolitan, People, The Cut,* and *Elle* are practically wall-papered with stories about royalty. Whatever William and Kate, or Harry and Meghan—or any other royals—are up to makes their pages. Nary a concern about the patriarchy tinges their reporting. Curiously, princess stories still sell, even among women who are "supposed to know better."

---

[7]   Jessie Bernard, *The Future of Marriage* (World Publishing, 1972), 48.

Tragically, the feminist solution to malcontent hasn't been a solution at all, as the statistics tell us. It has brought no relief to Betty Friedan's "ache that has no name." The ache is still alive and well, swelling wildly as women become more and more convinced that there is a cure for their malcontent somewhere out there.

Sadly, and most important for our understanding of what is truly going on, this dissatisfaction, this thirsting for more, this lack of contentment and discernment, this emotional wave, has opened up a most dramatic weak spot that the devil continues to exacerbate with designs of his own. The feminists are right: there is a cure. But their so-called enlightenment has blinded them to it and made their situation much worse.

CHAPTER 3

Goddess Worship Is Afoot

"Monotheism makes me grouchy. I don't trust any
religion that makes God look like one of the ruling
class. I guess I'm a pagan or an animist."

—Gloria Steinem

When looking at contemporary culture, it can be difficult to see any kind of a collective or orchestrated anti-Mary movement. Like scattershot, women appear to be acting badly independently of each other. What is not widely known are the anti-Marian roots that run deep in the goddess movement, also known as Wicca (or witchcraft). Goddess worship among pagans is a very ancient thing, but it is suddenly new and hip again, given new life with a fabricated narrative constructed in the 1970s. A current estimate of witches is around 1.5 million in the US, outpacing the 1.4 million mainline Presbyterians nationwide.[1] Where

---

[1] Michael W. Chapman, "Number of Witches in US on the Rise, May Surpass 1.5 Million," *CNS News*, November 16, 2018, https://www.cnsnews.com/blog/michael-w-chapman/number-witches-us-rise-may-outnumber-presbyterians.

there is goddess worship, radical feminism isn't far behind, and *vice versa.*

The contemporary story about goddess worship really only dates back to the 1970s, although promoters of it leave us with the impression that it is much older. Goddess worship, which is supposed to supplant the worship of a masculine God, rests upon the notion that before the patriarchy, matriarchies of women were in charge of things. Under the leadership of women, so the story goes, the world was peaceful, creative, beautiful, living in perfect harmony. With the arrival of the patriarchy, all of this changed; greed, violence, rape, and discord filled the earth. The goddess movement and goddess worship seek to restore the world to the harmony that existed under the matriarchy, particularly by helping women find "the goddess within"—their own special spark of divinity. A masculine God must be rejected because it is that model that brought about all the discord.

Women, according to the narrative, should be worshiped as divinities. Once a woman identifies her own goddess within, her moral decision-making will be led by "the goddess" through emotion and intuition, intense interior experiences, and "consciousness raising," instead of patriarchal enslavement to reason or logic. When the goddess movement has spread far enough, a New Age will be ushered in, offering perfect harmony between people and the environment. The rule by women will reclaim a balanced and serene existence among all of creation. "Only masculine ego," goddess movement author Elizabeth Gould Davis wrote, "stands in the way of decent society."[2] Lesbianism,

---

2   Elizabeth Gould Davis, *The First Sex* (Penguin, 1975), 35.

because it unites women together, is viewed as the highest form of sexual ideal. The sexual liberation of women is essential to the liberation of women and progress toward the matriarchal ideal.

There is at least one not-so-small problem with the goddess movement: it is built upon a bunch of nonsense. Cobbled together in the 1970s, the new religion of choice among radical feminism is built upon virtually no historical evidence that matriarchies were serene and harmonious utopias; in fact, there is plenty of evidence of the opposite, which we will see later. Books like *God is a Woman, The Spiral Dance: A Rebirth of the Ancient Religion of the Great Goddess, Dreaming in the Dark: Magic, Sex and Politics*, and *Womanspirit Rising* are all a mishmash of pagan religions, sexual liberation, and misanthropy—guided by the principle articulated by one member: "Remember. Make an effort to remember. Or, failing that, invent."[3] Truth, logic, and reason are the enemy. Invention (fabrication, lies) are good too because truth is of little value. Nothing, certainly not the truth, can stand in the way of the narrative.

Divinizing women, promoting lesbianism, abandoning logic and reason, and lying should be enough to make the connection between the goddess movement and an anti-Marian spirit clear. Unfortunately, this movement isn't limited to a small cabal of witches; it has much longer tentacles.

---

[3]   Monique Wittig, quoted by Philip G. Davis, *Goddess Unmasked* (Spence Publishing, 1998), 53.

Culture Awash in the Goddess

Knowledge of myths and biblical stories of old are meant to be informative and help us understand human nature, which is why children are often encouraged to learn Greek myths or other types of mythology. This new focus upon goddesses, however, isn't about accurately depicting these ancient stories to teach ancient truths but re-presenting them in new packaging to appeal to modern feminist women. Mythical women of every stripe have been rebranded for contemporary use. Wicca has claimed to be following the lead of the goddess Diana or Artemis. *Jezebel,* once the name of the murderous Old Testament queen, is now an edgy online magazine. And Lilith—a night demon of old—became patroness of Lilith Fair, a music festival for female musical artists, and the Lilith Fund, established for women to get abortions after Hurricane Harvey struck Houston in 2017. The infiltration of the goddess movement has been subtle, so subtle that most have missed it, but slowly our culture has become awash in goddess emulation and worship. Even Jennifer Aniston has bought into it: "You know when I feel inwardly beautiful? When I am with my girlfriends and we are having a 'goddess circle.'"[4]

The music industry offers some of the most blatant examples of the power of the goddess movement among us today. Madonna has perhaps done the most to entrench the anti-Mary/goddess worship ideal into our culture. The first and most obvious thing she did was to rebrand the name

---

[4]   Jennifer Aniston (@xjenniferanistonx), Instagram, January 2, 2017.

Madonna. Prior to Madonna Louise Ciccone's arrival onto the music scene, the name Madonna was holy and belonged uniquely to Our Lady. Madonna Louise tarnished the brand. *Badly*. Even her confirmation name is rich with irony; it is Veronica, which means "true image," referring to the cloth that Veronica used to wipe Christ's face when he was on the Way of the Cross. With her boytoy persona, consistent vulgarity, over-cooked sensuality, and foray into desecrating religious themes, she looks like a good anti-Marian pin-up (or mug shot?). But all of that was surpassed by her 2013 Super Bowl Halftime Show where she pulled out all of the sacrilegious stops by performing the equivalent of a twelve-minute satanic ritual. Before the event, she told Anderson Cooper, "The Super Bowl is kind of like the Holy of Holies in America. I'll come at halfway of the 'church experience' and I'm gonna have to deliver a sermon. It'll have to be very impactful."[5] Her detailed performance was not just another Hollywood production but carefully orchestrated to include satanic and pagan symbols of divinity.

Madonna isn't the only musician to "channel" goddesses. Beyoncé followed the "Queen of Pop" in her own appearances, dressing as Youruba goddess Yeye Oshun—the goddess of fertility, motherhood, and passing generations. She imitated this goddess at the 2017 Grammys when she was pregnant with twins, identifying further with the Nigerian goddess, who is said to have also given birth to twins.

---

[5]   Madonna, "Madonna is Nervous About Super Bowl Performance," interview with Anderson Cooper, January 31, 2012, https://www.youtube.com/watch?v=ZMaMQoHpQyo.

Pop artist Rihanna has said that Madonna is her biggest influence, idolizing her because of her capacity to constantly reinvent herself. Rihanna is hoping to be named the "black Madonna." Yet again, a pop star is trying to claim another of Our Lady's titles, while whittling away at any remaining moral fabric of the culture.

Not to be left out as a goddess groupie, pop sensation Ariana Grande released a song in 2018 called "God is a Woman." The song details the sexual relationship between a man and a woman, where the woman claims to be God because of all the pleasure she can bring him. The lyrics—too explicit to print—even compares having illicit sexual relations to praying, just to make sure the sacrilege is perfectly clear.

The Woman of Folly

Anti-Marian archetypes are rife in Scripture and literature. Scripture makes it clear that there is a type of woman who needs to be avoided, whose influence will always lead to bad places. Eve is certainly the primal example, with Jezebel, Salome, and the Whore of Babylon as other standouts. The book of Proverbs speaks of the Woman of Folly, who promises life but leads to death. Here is one warning:

> Saving you from a stranger,
> from a foreign woman with her smooth words,
> One who forsakes the companion of her youth
> and forgets the covenant of her God;
> For her path sinks down to death,
> and her footsteps lead to the shades.
> None who enter there come back,
> or gain the paths of life. (Prv 2:16–19 NABRE)

And another: "Wisdom builds her house but Folly tears hers down with her own hands" (Prv 14:1).

The woman of folly inflicts gross spiritual and physical damage. Her toxicity spreads like a cancer on a soul and society. She is manipulative, deceitful, deceptive, seductive, and narcissistic. She quietly destroys others with a smile on her face and nary a prick to her conscience. She teaches others to do the same, enthralling and entrapping them with her beauty, her aloof sophistication, and her faux kindness. Sirens, gorgons, harpies, Scylla, Medusa, Echidna, Astarte, Lamia, and Isis are among the scores of women of folly that come down to us through mythology and literature. Two others, in particular, serve as the most prominent women of folly archetypes, two whose vices seem to be making further in-roads today and who serve as broader categories for us to put the rest into and show us all the ways women can go wrong: Jezebel and Lilith.

Jezebel

Sin is, as the Church has told us for millennia, banal and uncreative, so those who are enslaved by it have very little room to differentiate themselves from others. For this reason, so many women of folly will remind us of Jezebel.

Featured in the first book of Kings, Jezebel was the queen of Israel as the wife of King Ahab. Although evil before marrying her, under her influence, Ahab came to serve and worship the god of Baal. He became a passive and controlled subject in his own kingdom, while Jezebel ruthlessly murdered true prophets and upheld soothsayers. When Ahab was sullen that Naboth, a vineyard owner, would not sell Ahab his vineyard, Jezebel took matters into her own hands and had Naboth stoned to death. Eventually, Ahab repented of his wrongdoing, but Jezebel did not. For her transgressions, she was eventually thrown out of a window to her death, where her body was eaten by dogs.

There are other mythological characters who have this similar spirit. One is called Le-hev-hev, a name that means "that which draws us to it so that it may devour us."[6] This Jezebel spirit can be seen in Salome, the wife of Herod, who had her daughter ask for the head of John the Baptist on a platter. A common characteristic is that a Jezebel type will enslave or trap her prey and then devour it, much like a black widow spider. J. R. R. Tolkien used the image of a ruthless spider as the guard of Mordor, Shelob, a female spider who paralyzes and then devours her prey (it was Galadriel's light—a symbol of Mary—that saved Frodo and Sam from the voracious spider).

A richer description of the manipulation of a Jezebel spirit includes confusion, intimidation, draining the opposition through argumentation, refusing facts, changing the subject when proven wrong, blaming others for her faults, use of pseudo-friendships to acquire favors and accrue power, and eventually conquering the opposition through destruction or betrayal. Like King Ahab, Adam, Herod, and others, men under the spell of a Jezebel tend to give way to her cunning, while becoming passively open to her vicious whims. The

---

6   Erich Neumann, *The Great Mother* (Princeton University Press, 2015), 174.

goddess movement espouses many of these characteristics, particularly the way it denies the importance of truth, denigrates the virtues of men, and divinizes women.

Lilith

In the 1960s, Anton LaVey, considered the father of Satanism and dubbed the "Black pope," predicted that the year 1966 would usher in the age of Satan or, more specifically, the age of Lilith. While the word of a Satanist shouldn't hold much stock, if we look back at the last fifty years, there certainly has been an uptick in the demonic, specifically that of targeting women and the resurgence of the cult of Lilith.

But who is this Lilith? She has been called the wife of Satan and a blood-sucking night demon. James Joyce called her the patroness of abortion, and she has been featured in the work of Victor Hugo, as well as that of George MacDonald in his book *Lilith, A Romance*. C. S. Lewis used her as his model for Jadis, the White Witch, and even Michelangelo drew her as a temptress in the Garden of Eden. Exorcists warn of her, and rituals abound historically to protect against her. Even the word *lullaby* comes from the Arabic words meaning "beware of Lilith." Despite all this, few today have any idea who she is.

Her story has been told around hearths and firesides for millennia. First mentioned in *The Epic of Gilgamesh*, the legends about her predate Genesis, and millennia-old cave carvings of her have been found in Egypt, Sumeria, Babylonia, and Greece. She is often depicted as an owl because she works at night, or as a large-breasted woman with owls at her feet. In every mythological story, she is an evil woman, a demon, or a monstrous creature. She is the terror of the night. Her name stems from the ancient Sumerian word for female demon or wind spirits and she is said to dwell in the desert.

Other attributes include preying mostly upon infants and pregnant women, breasts that are filled with poison instead of milk, and seducing men in their sleep (one variation of her name describes an infertile and sexually frustrated woman who aggressively pursues young men, which also has a familiar ring in our day). In short, she embodies chaos, destruction, and ungodliness.

Lilith appears once in Scripture in the book of Isaiah. As the Old Testament book explains, Yahweh is going to smite the land of Edom and it will become a sterile desert, with roaming wild animals. "Wildcats shall meet desert beasts, satyrs shall call to one another; There shall the lilith repose, and find for herself a place to rest" (Is 34:14 NABRE). It's clear that Isaiah and those to whom he is writing are aware of who Lilith is and that she is not a sign of God's favor. "The wilderness traditionally symbolizes mental and physical barrenness; it is a place where creativity and life itself are easily extinguished. Lilith, the feminine opposite of masculine order, is banished from fertile territory and exiled to barren wasteland."[7] Lilith resides in this barren place of doom.

Lilith's story took on new energy sometime between the eighth and tenth centuries in the book *Alphabet of Ben Sira*.

---

7   Janet Howe Gaines, "Lilith," *Biblical History Daily*, March 15, 2018, https://www.biblicalarchaeology.org/daily/people-cultures-in-the-bible/people-in-the-bible/lilith/.

The anonymous text was written to reconcile the apparent inconsistency in Scripture between the two stories of the creation of man and woman in Genesis 1 and 2. In Genesis 1, the *Alphabet* proposes, the first man and first woman, Adam and Lilith, were created at the same time and immediately started fighting for supremacy. Lilith, refusing to submit to Adam, stomps out of the Garden of Eden. She then blasphemes God, gets banished from Eden altogether, and turns into a winged devil. As a further punishment, one hundred of her children are to be killed each day. She lives out her vengeance through the seduction of men to bolster her own fertility, while wantonly killing infants who have not been protected against her.

In the 1800s, Lilith was still considered dark and evil and garnered little sympathy, with the exception of George Mac-Donald's prior mentioned novel, *Lilith: A Romance*, where he stretches the imagination to see if Christ can redeem even her. But the truly evil spirit of Lilith is certainly alive today in the reality of children killed through abortion, abuse, or neglect. And the seduction of men by women has become so commonplace, aided by the accessibility of contraception and abortion, that it is just part of the culture. The hook-up culture and shows like *Sex and the City* or *Girls* that glamorize the lifestyle of "going through men" have made heterosexual sin so banal that more exotic forms of eroticism have become trendy, particularly homosexuality, which opened wide the doors to the now readily accepted LGBT movement.

Today, there are whole collections of Lilith books, racy paperbacks, dark novels, films, music, video games with demonic imagery, obscenity, et cetera, all presented in a "fun" and less threatening manner, yet no less destructive (and perhaps more so). She is now seen to be a noble goddess, who stands up to the patriarchy while endorsing lesbianism, eroticism, and the whole sordid mess.

All of these elements which describe Jezebel and Lilith culminate in the terrible woman represented in Revelation: the Whore of Babylon. Although said to be a woman in the future, she embodies the best of female vice, making her the worst. She doesn't just reject purity and motherhood; she murders her children and then gets drunk on their blood. Her vices are used to dominate and destroy men, like the devouring spider or murderous Jezebel:

> "The kings of the earth have had intercourse with her, and the inhabitants of the earth became drunk on the wine of her harlotry." Then he carried me away in spirit to a deserted place where I saw a woman seated on a scarlet beast that was covered with blasphemous names, with seven heads and ten horns. The woman was wearing purple and scarlet and adorned with gold, precious stones, and pearls. She held in her hand a gold cup that was filled with the abominable and sordid deeds of her harlotry. On her forehead was written a name, which is a mystery, "Babylon the great, the mother of harlots and of the abominations of the earth." I saw that the woman was drunk on the blood of the holy ones and on the blood of the witnesses to Jesus. (Rv 17:2–6 NABRE)

Fifty years ago, such a woman was nearly inconceivable, but after the damage wrought during the past decades, the Whore of Babylon now has a familiar ring.

Exorcists Weigh In

Myth and Scripture are not the only places we can find Jezebel and Lilith; they can also be found in the arena of exorcism.

Fr. Gabriele Amorth, who served as the Vatican's chief exorcist and the honorary president of the International Association of Exorcists until he passed away in 2016, is said to have "exorcised Lilith, Beelzebub, and Lucifer and other demons so often now that he feels he can recognize them right at the start of an exorcism."[8] Exorcist Fr. Chad Ripperger has also exorcised the demon of Lilith, whom he describes as "one of the top five, very strong and difficult to get out."[9] Ironically, for all the adulation given to Lilith by radical feminists, Fr. Ripperger explains that "demons are not female but only appear as such." He adds, "Demons do not have a gender but always appear as male except when they are trying to seduce in some manner."[10] Lilith fits this exception. Father explains, "It is a him that acts like a her. He manifests as male except when trying to convince others that he is a she for some nefarious purpose." There is plenty

---

[8]   Alastair Wickham, *The Dead Roam the Earth* (Penguin Books, 2012), 253.

[9]   Chad Ripperger, email exchange with author, July and August 2018.

[10]   Ibid.

of irony in feminists worshipping a demon they believe is female but actually manifests as a male.

As for Jezebel, Fr. Ripperger also confirmed that there is a demonic spirit connected to her. Jezebel, Fr. Ripperger explains, "is a spirit which seeks to undermine authority structures through women primarily, though not exclusively, in which murmuring is used to undermine the authority."[11] She attacks "right order in governance within families, communities, organizations."[12]

Demons, in general, do not have the capacity to influence the wider culture if people are not first complicit in sin. For these anti-Marian spirits to gain a foothold in the culture, men and women had to open the door through their own sinfulness, stepping outside of the state of grace, which allowed the demonic to enter into a soul in one form or another. Fr. Ripperger reports, "I tend to find that various demons tend to use the disorders of Original Sin that are proper to women, for example, the desire for self-sufficiency separate from one's husband, the desire to control, the fear of being hurt, etc. Demons just make hay out of these matters and have gained great ascendancy in our culture."[13]

Cautionary Tales

Putting aside exorcists and the sensational, there is much more to ancient mythical stories than mere storytelling, as we saw in the last chapter. These stories have an important

---

[11]   Ibid.
[12]   Ibid.
[13]   Ibid.

place for teaching us how we ought to live. The Lilith story told by the Jews in the Middle Ages was not meant to be a story of female triumph and empowerment, as many see it now. Instead, it was a cautionary tale of what happens when the proper authority of man over women is disrupted. Everyone loses under this arrangement, for reasons that we shall see in more depth in part 2.

So why is it that these types of stories have been so often repeated from time immemorial? Because the telling of these kinds of stories offers wisdom about how women can and should avoid becoming like Lilith, Jezebel, or Eve. They also help us to recognize the difference between men and women, that women have a different set of gifts to offer the world than men do.

These ancient scary stories were retold as collective wisdom about what not to do, but with the arrival of Christianity, the stories took on a new cast. No longer limited to scary storytelling, with the arrival of Christ and the Blessed Mother, men and women had role models to follow, not just demons to avoid. Cautionary tales no longer had to be about bad women, but transitioned into how to emulate good women, particularly, the greatest woman of all: Mary, the Mother of God. Both kinds of storytelling helped form cultures that understood—at the very least—the important of roles of men and women.

For many generations, as Christianity has grown more threadbare, folktales and myths are rarely told in their original teaching form. Western culture has been left without the wisdom of old once presented through the medium of story. The affect has been that women of the 1960s forward believed that they were doing something new, something revolutionary. Lacking any sort of collective memory about how they ought to live for peace and harmony, the result was to fall directly back into the hornet's nest of problems that civilizations in the past warned against. In thinking that they were being wise and innovative, radical feminists and their daughters and granddaughters became the new women of folly.

PART II

Anti-Mary, Inc.

CHAPTER 4

The Big Lie: Changing Human Nature

"I don't really view communism as a bad thing."

—Whoopi Goldberg

In 1917, during one of Our Lady's apparitions at Fatima, the three shepherd children were given a vision of hell. Our Lady warned that if people didn't stop offending God, then another war would come. In reparation, Our Lady asked "for the consecration of Russia to my Immaculate Heart, and the Communion of reparation on the First Saturdays." She added, "If my requests are heeded, Russia will be converted, and there will be peace; if not, she will spread her errors throughout the world, causing wars and persecutions of the Church."[1]

---

[1]   Joseph Cardinal Ratzinger, "The Message of Fatima," Congregation for the Doctrine of Faith, http://www.vatican.va/roman_curia/congregations/cfaith/documents/rc_con_cfaith_doc_20000626_message-fatima_en.html.

What, then, were the errors of Russia that she was referring to? Most of us think of Russian errors largely as communist and Marxist ideologies. This is generally correct, as Marxism is behind most of the ideologies we face today either openly or surreptitiously, be it communism, collectivism, or socialism. But could there be more to it than just that? Something deeper than Marx and his fellow comrades?

Russia's Errors

In 1918, shortly after Our Lady's prediction, Tsar Nicolas Romanov and his entire family were shot, bayonetted, and clubbed to death. Their bodies were dragged to a desolate forest, where they were further mutilated and finally thrown down a mineshaft. With the royal family gone, the Bolsheviks, led by Vladimir Lenin, expanded his party's controlling power over the expansive Russian Empire. Lenin made his intentions of massive cultural overhaul very plain:

> We are . . . the real revolutionaries—yes, we are going to tear the whole thing down! We shall destroy and smash everything, ha-ha-ha, with the result that everything will be smashed to smithereens and fly off in all directions, and nothing will remain standing!
>
> Yes, we are going to destroy everything, and on the ruins we will build our temple! It will be a temple for the happiness of all! But we shall destroy the entire bourgeoisie, and grind them to powder—ha-ha-ha— to powder. Remember that![2]

---

[2]   Warren H. Carroll, *1917 Red Banners, White Mantle* (Front Royal, VA: Christendom Publications, 1981), 120.

Under the Soviet tyranny, private property became a thing of the past and the aristocracy was neutralized (or vaporized) by exile at the Gulag work camps. Their property was seized, their homes were divided up to share with strangers, or they were harassed until "charges" could be brought up justifying execution. For the commoners—the proletariat who were supposed to be the beneficiaries of Soviet collectivization—breadlines, hunger, and the unraveling of society became the new norm. The family was destroyed as all adults were forced to work, children were raised by others, and divorce was easily procured. The Orthodox Christian faith was erased as churches were converted into store houses and museums, or simply destroyed. When battering rams knocked down the doors of the iconic church of Our Lady of Kazan, loudspeakers blared, "You see, there is no God! We destroy the church of the so-called protectress of Russia and nothing happens!"

Anyone objecting to the new Soviet "utopia" was sent, along with priests and aristocrats, to the Gulag, where an estimated forty to sixty million people perished from disease, malnourishment, exposure, torture, and execution.

At the heart of Marxist ideology was the goal to remake human nature and human society in such a way that everyone was equal—or the same—by trying to erase every natural or societal difference. Aristotle, millennia before, had warned against such foolishness: "The worst form of inequality is to try to make unequal things equal." While masquerading as healthy egalitarianism with ambitious goals for every comrade, the stratified Russian culture quickly became a country of two classes: those in power (with resources taken from others) and those not in power (with very few resources). Envy and power-seeking (and hunger) became the powerful emotions fueling Soviet communism. Within a decade, the Soviet economy was transformed from a fertile bread basket to an anemic display of what happens when no one owns anything.

Women's liberation, the Bolsheviks believed, was completely tied to the success of communism. Russian revolutionary Inessa Armand emphasized this point in one pithy quote: "If women's liberation is unthinkable without communism, then communism is unthinkable without women's liberation."[3] It was imperative that the idea of motherhood was divorced from the reality of being a woman. The official party position was stated by Aleksandra Kollentai, the head of the Soviet "Women's Department," who said, "The shackles of the family, of the housework, of prostitution still weigh heavily on the working woman. Working women and peasant women can only rid themselves of this situation and achieve equality in life itself, and not just in law, if they put all their energies into making Russia a truly communist society."[4] The Bolsheviks severed the tie between motherhood and womanhood. These same ideas would be echoed by the women's liberation movement in the West several decades later.

---

[3]   Sharon Smith, "Women's Liberation: The Marxist Tradition," *International Socialist Review* no. 93, https://isreview.org/issue/93/womens-liberation-marxist-tradition.

[4]   Quoted in Kengor, *Takedown*, 39, Aleksandra Kollentai, "International Women's Day," *International Socialist Review*, January-February 2012, 29–34.

The Soviets worked quickly to legalize abortion to make women equal to men, and then they put the women to work. As author Paul Kengor wrote, "You weren't free to own a farm or factory or business or bank account or go to church or print your own newspaper, but if you wanted a divorce or abortion, the sky was the limit in Bolshevik Russia."[5] With abortion free and legal, it spread like wildfire among the population. In 1934, abortions outweighed live births by three to one. Only later, when the Soviets eventually realized their self-created birth-dearth was leading to massive demographic problems (much like China today), did policy changes come about that incentivized having children.

The Soviets, not content with their own borders, sought to take over neighboring countries. Though mostly thwarted before the Second World War, they were victorious in taking over numerous satellite countries as their spoils from the war, including Poland, Ukraine, Bulgaria, Latvia, Georgia, Romania, Hungary, East Germany, and Czechoslovakia. Behind this new "Iron Curtain," these once vibrant countries were stuffed into the gray ill-fitting militant uniform required by the Soviets. Faith was clandestine, friends turned on each other in an instant, and everyone—friend, foe, or family—was a "comrade."

The Russian Revolution unleashed the idea that human nature is infinitely malleable and can be rearranged into perfect equality. People who lived under the Soviet shadow paid a horrendous price. Since nature (and all that is natural) manifests a great deal of inequality, Lenin *et al* had

---

[5]   Kengor, *Takedown*, 34.

to tear it all down. The natural and the supernatural orders were the real obstacles that had to be destroyed. It is almost impossible to describe the widespread devastation these errors brought to the people of Russia and beyond. The scars are still readily apparent amid the people, the land, and the faith. Vicki Thorn, founder of Project Rachel, reports that one woman admitted having eighty abortions. Thorn, having never heard of such a high number, first had to consult a doctor to verify that such a number was even physically possible. Yes, the doctor said, and not as uncommon as one might think.

Russia's Errors Spread

Ryszard Legutko, a Polish Member of the European Parliament and university professor, grew up under Soviet communism. He saw his beloved Krakow, the cultural capital of Poland, reduced to a dreary state of grey crumbling buildings—buildings that had once boasted of bright yellows, greens, and orange—while churches were left in disrepair and the infrastructure cracked underfoot. The rot of the city served, as much as anything, as a reminder of the spiritual rot growing in the souls of so many. Millions were poisoned by the communist ideology and were left in isolation, afraid of family and neighbor alike, fearing that any human contact with their comrades could be used against them by the government.

Legutko, like most Poles, was thrilled to see the fall of the Iron Curtain. He was enthralled by the freedom ushered into Poland by the West when the Soviets finally closed up what was left of the shop. As he watched Poland transition from the old communist way of doing things to adopt Western practices and ideas, he was left with a nagging question. How is it, he asked, that Poles who had been staunch Soviet "comrades" so quickly and smoothly transitioned into European liberals? Legutko wonders, in his book *The Demon of Democracy: Totalitarian Temptations in Free Societies*, if the two projects were diametrically opposed, shouldn't there have been more of struggle from one to the other.[6] Legutko concludes that the reason the former communists easily leapt from one ideology to the next was that, at their core, they were actually the same ideology; both were committed to making a complete break with the past and with tradition, particularly the Church; both looked toward progress to lead to the perfect man, the perfect society; and both found ways to silence those who thwarted their goals, particularly through media control and "newspeak." Both, at their core, were committed to changing human nature.

In comparing the two ideologies, Legutko further explains their commonalities:

> By becoming a member of a communist and liberal-democratic society, man rejects a vast share of loyalties and commitments that until not long ago shackled him, in particular those that were imposed on him through the tutelage of religion, social morality, and tradition. He feels renewed and strong and therefore has nothing but pity toward those miserable ones

---

6   Ryszard Legutko, *The Demon in Democracy* (Encounter Books, 2018).

who continue to be attached to long-outdated rules and who succumb to the bondage of unreasonable restraints.

But there is one obligation from which he cannot be relieved: for a communist, communism, and for a liberal democrat, liberal democracy. These obligations are non-negotiable. Others can be ignored.[7]

The false premise animating both ideologies is that human nature can be changed. Progress toward a utopian goal is measured by how many people have taken on this new human nature. Their belief is that once the process is complete, and this new nature is assumed by all, then there will be worldwide happiness. Until then, "we have to break a few eggs." The only foreseeable solution from their viewpoint is contained in an unwavering adherence to the party. Should ideological faults be exposed (like famine, misery, chaos, etc.), blame is pinned on the fact that the ideology hasn't been embraced by everyone. "It only works if everyone does it," is their false argument.

The Sadness of Demons

Legutko's insight about the effort to change human nature isn't just limited to contemporary ideologies but has a much longer history. In writing about demons, St. Thomas Aquinas says, "Now it is evident that the demons would wish many things not to be, which are, and others to be, which are not: for, out of envy, they would wish others to be

---

7   Ibid.

damned, who are saved" (I, Q64.3). Among their sufferings, the demons have a type of eternal sadness because they cannot change human nature. Psychologist Fr. Mike Driscoll says, "Demons are forever unhappy . . . because they want God's creation to be different than it is, and they will never succeed in changing it to their liking."[8]

It is curious, then, to consider that this eternal sadness of demons is connected with their desire to change human nature. It is not surprising that the ideologies emanating from "Russia's errors" also have this same fundamental thrust toward changing human nature. This perversion of human nature is at the heart of the errors Our Lady talked about at Fatima.

The errors of Russia, which have spread well beyond her borders, are ultimately that they try to do what the devil desires: change human nature. But this cannot be done. Thus, the demons are sad in the face of the impossible task, and those infected with Russia's errors rage and destroy everything that isn't to their liking, as seen in the anti-Marian spirit.

The Errors Go Viral

The errors Our Lady alluded to aren't exclusive to Russia and Europe. The promises of the Russian Revolution—that human nature can be changed—melted seamlessly into the promises of the sexual revolution. Americans have widely adopted the notion that human nature is infinitely malleable,

---

8   Fr. Mike Driscoll, *Demons, Deliverance, Discernment*, Catholic Answers Press, 2015, Kindle Edition.

that a mother, for example, could willingly and pridefully kill her own child, that spouses could forsake each other with the expectation that there will be no consequences to themselves or their children, or that men could lie with each other and expect an open embrace from all and sundry. From the 1960s on, each of these erroneous concepts aimed at appeasing the desires of the human heart have failed miserably to serve the individual, the family, or the wider common good.

It is no accident that the ideology of Soviet communism blended comfortably with the egalitarianism of the sexual revolution. French intellectual and author of *The Second Sex* Simon Beauvoir considered one of the real triumphs of Soviet Russia to be women's liberation from menial tasks at home. Radical feminist Shulamith Firestone took it one step further when she wrote feverishly about eliminating gender differences. "The end goal of the feminist revolution must be, unlike that of the first feminist movement, not just the elimination of male *privilege* but of the sex *distinction* itself: genital differences between human beings would no longer matter culturally."[9] The thrust behind feminist ideology is that in order for men and women to have equal treatment, they must become exactly the same. Any sort of difference must be overlooked. We have to ignore the fact that women have babies and are physically weaker on the whole than men. We have to ignore the fact that transgendered men who transition to women are really not women, and we have to ignore the fact that there is no physical way that two men

---

9   Shulamith Firestone, *The Dialectic of Sex: The Case for Feminist Revolution* (New York: William Morrow and Company, 1970), 11.

can have a baby, even if they feel entitled to parenthood and at any cost. Like communism before it, all differences in reality must be overlooked to conform to the ideological narrative.

Radical feminism regularly promotes the "nature can be changed" lie, with celebrities proclaiming that gender equality is the "emergency of our time" that must be addressed with frantic (and vulgar) urgency. Their breathless exhortations are littered with the same type of newspeak used in the Soviet Union. Words and expressions such as pro-choice, a woman's right to choose, reproductive rights, termination of pregnancy, clump of cells, product of conception, anti-abortion, and anti-choice all cover up the reality of which they speak. Such false realities have misled many, including an article in *Elle* that expressed shock over an ultrasound image that looked more like a real baby than fetuses do in an "actual" pregnancy (because they are thought to just be a clump of cells).

Our infinitely changing human nature has made both men and women obsolete. Men have become unnecessary and even the enemy because "the future is female." Of course, in reality, there won't be an exclusively female future—whatever that might mean—unless they mean that the usual method of achieving pregnancy is abandoned and that only little girls are born through innovative scientific means. And yet, somehow, there seems to be the impression that this could happen and that it would be a good thing. Elsewhere, women have become unnecessary because of the "changes" in nature. Among homosexual men, including those embedded in the Church, women are superfluous. For homosexuals, clerics and otherwise, the complementarity of male and female is outmoded or unimportant for society to function properly. Women are as useful to homosexuals as "a bicycle is to a fish."[10]

Jesuit priest Fr. James Martin furthers the error when he recommends that homosexuality no longer be referred to as intrinsically disordered but rebranded as "differently ordered." He is, yet again, trying to tweak human nature to include naturally sterile and supernaturally prohibited sexual acts.

Both of these ideologies—radical feminism and homosexuality—are committing the same error of negating the necessity and goodness of the opposite sex. Neither has a use for healthy, ordered, loving men and women, parents, and children. They want the world and the Church to be ruled by "the new men and women" with a "new human nature" who are sterile in word and in deed.

Russia's errors are reverberating through the highest levels of the cultural and clerical elite. Like the demons before them, they are determined to destroy the faith and the fundamental building block of a flourishing society: the family.

---

10   A famous quote attributed to feminist Gloria Steinem, although first coined by Irina Dunn.

A not unimportant piece of information about the women who think the "future is female" is that almost all of these "mothers" of the feminist movement had deep issues with their own mothers, as we will see in the next chapter. And homosexual men, as psychologist Joseph Nicolosi and others have pointed out, generally have deep issues with their fathers. While not entirely reducible to parenting, there is a piece of the problem that is largely overlooked: healthy and good moms and dads.

More Lies: Women Aren't Mothers

The Soviet Revolution and the subsequent sexual revolution presented the world with another new idea, another lie based upon the original lie that human nature can change. They introduced into society the notion that a new kind of woman could exist, the anti-Marian woman. No longer was every woman required to accept motherhood of some sort, but women were given the capacity to somehow step out of the confines of motherhood. This break from motherhood freed a woman to finally be who she truly is—she could be a reporter, a CEO, a Marine, or even morph into something altogether different: *she* could become a *he*. For women to consider themselves mothers was no longer part of their biological hardwiring or of their thinking because it was no longer part of their being. Motherhood was accidental to what it means to be a woman—it could happen or not, but it didn't touch the core of who a woman was.

In the book *The Great Mother*, psychologist Erich Neumann digs deeply into myths and ancient stories that depict women and goddesses. One of the main themes that emerges about women is that we are vessels. We have wombs that carry and protect children and we carry in our hearts and minds the needs and being of others. The physical reality of pregnancy and childbearing is duplicated in our souls on a spiritual level. So even if a woman is not a biological mother, she is still naturally oriented toward "mothering" others—by gifting herself for the care and welfare of others.

As Neumann discusses, women carry the needs, hopes, fears, anxiety, and love of others. We also marinate and ruminate about our loved ones in an effort to make their lives better. For this reason, in stories and myths, women are symbolized by such things as a vessel, a ship, the ocean, an oven, or even a coffin. Cities, too, the place where people gather for care and safety, are mostly thought of in the feminine, as is evident particularly in the romance languages. Even the Church is referred to as a *she*. Architecturally, the largest space in a church is called a "nave," referring again to a ship. Throughout human history, this element of "containment" has been inseparable from what it means to be a woman; that is, until the last century.

In light of this essential capacity of women to contain others, Neumann evaluates female figures drawn from across history on how they manage the charges put into their care. Are they gentle and loving mothers or murderous and dangerous? Do they help others grow, or do they cut them down and dissolve their personality? Neumann concludes that we can characterize a woman based on how she treats those entrusted to her. The terrible mother, according to Neumann, is that woman who abhors life and tries to destroy it when she can, including by dismemberment for ritual sacrifice. The bad mother is the one who controls those she is given power over. She manipulates her children, leaving them in a state of dependency so that she is always in control and they are locked in an infantile or undeveloped state. The good and great mothers are on the sliding scale of nurturing those in their care. Like a steady gardener, this mother knows the correct balance of love, affection, and engagement to allow a child to ultimately become free of her. Her job, when done well, is to make herself all but obsolete. The difference between the good and the great mother is a woman's capacity to raise a fully mature and flourishing adult.

Neumann provides an amazing circular chart where major female types and goddesses are placed respectively in the position of a terrible, bad, good, or great mother. All women can be considered within this circle. There is a place for Lilith, Circe, Astarte, Kali, Demeter, Sophia, Isis, and even the Virgin Mary. Again, each has a place based on her tending to human souls.

The comprehensive nature of Neumann's analysis helps reveal the lie that, somehow because of contraception and abortion, women can evade their innate maternal nature. The true reality is that these elements do not mean that we have stepped out of motherhood. But contemporary women, because of their active efforts to destroy the life of their children, have gone from good or great mothers to mimicking the bad or terrible mothers. Perhaps we are too close to see this sorry state, but future generations who have recaptured some sense of sanity will see clearly that our age was the age of the terrible mother. We didn't step out of our fertility (because that is ontologically impossible), we just stepped into a terrible way to manage that which we were tasked with "containing."

Although Neumann does not lay his analysis out this way, there is added clarity in understanding his point by using Aristotle's ancient criteria of a virtue. Aristotle saw that the way to establish a virtuous act is to find the "golden mean," that spot in the middle of two extreme vices. If we look at the two kinds of extremes that women are tempted to—overcontrol, on one side, and negligence, on the other—then we can see that the virtuous woman is the one who balances these two extremes. It's easy to think of the domineering and manipulative mother, on one hand, or the negligent and narcissistic mother, on the other, who can't be bothered with her family's needs. In the middle of these two is the good or great mother who is nurturing, supportive, attentive, and selfless.

Despite our contemporary misreading of human nature, there is simply no way for a woman to take herself out of motherhood. Everything she is or does is, in essence, somehow related to her embrace or rejection of it. Women are made for motherhood, so our stewardship of life and the quality of our character can be judged on how we engage in it. This is the way human nature is hardwired, and everything in our bodies speaks to this truth—in our hips, in our wombs, in our arms that are bent at the elbow (instead of straight like men's) to better cradle a child, in our breasts which offer nourishment, and so on. We can reject this reality, we can wish it weren't so, but we cannot escape it.

Even that woman who undergoes surgery to transition into a "male," at her core, is still a woman made for mothering. One hundred years from now, her bones will tell the real story, and there will be no sign left that she was a *he* because her hips and arms are still those of a woman, and her proportions will still be female. Try as we might to change her sex, or "unsex" her, as Lady MacBeth dared request, we cannot truly succeed. The natural order simply cannot be changed, no matter how sad or angry that fact makes some.

The Lie that Traps

Communism, Marxism, socialism, and radical feminism all share a remarkable pedigree of failure when it comes to human happiness, and yet we continue trying them with the expectation that the results will somehow be different. The newspeak may be different, the language and the laws enacted by it may be different, but their appeal is based upon the big lie that human nature can be changed, and once it is, the world will be perfect.

What few realize is that the actions associated with changing human nature have a built-in trap. They have a secret capacity to enslave their adherents with the mental-handcuffs of collaboration. The communists controlled party members by making them complicit in seizing property or betraying friends and family. The abortion movement, too, is counting on men and women who have been complicit in abortions to defend it. Intellectually and morally trapped, followers are stuck defending their own actions, wittingly or not, because they have been engaged in the destructive behavior that fuels their movement.

These are the errors of Russia that now enslave us the world-over.

CHAPTER 5

The Anti-Marian Architects

"A housewife's work has no results: it simply has to be done again. Bringing up children is not a real occupation, because children come up just the same, brought up or not."

—Germaine Greer

There is something striking about the speed at which the sexual revolution happened, which feminists often considered to be a sign of divinity behind their effort. The swiftness parallels the rapidness with which the Russian Revolution happened; in just a few short months in 1918, the tsar and his descendants were gone, and the Bolsheviks took over. As if overnight, everything changed. A small mob of communists, or in this case, feminists, turned everything on its head.

The 1960s were heady days for feminists. Phyllis Chesler argues that feminism happened overnight, saying, "We— who only yesterday had been viewed as cunts, whores, dykes, bitches, witches, and madwomen; we who had been second- and third-class citizens—had suddenly become players in history. The world would never be the same, and neither would we."[1]

Elite and savvy women arrived on the scene at the same time television was swaying the hearts and minds of Western culture. Women like the fiery Betty Friedan, the bold Gloria Steinem, and the saucy Helen Gurley Brown became the "it" women. They came along and filled the vacuum that had been left by the disintegration of true religious faith in the lives of everyday women. These elite women learned to control and manipulate the message that went out to women in such a way that their legacy holds strong today. There is not one major power corridor inhabited by women in the West—from Hollywood, to the fashion industry, to politics, to book publishing—that is not controlled by radical feminist women.

There is much more to their story, however, than just savvy media marketing and a timely message. The darker side to feminists' meteoric rise to stardom is rarely discussed. Despite appearances, these women who looked to be healthy, sexy, happy, and rich weren't all that the cameras made them out to be.

Feminism Didn't Come Out of Nowhere

Radical feminism isn't something that happened quite as overnight as it appears. Its roots reach back a long way. Two world wars prompted the collateral damage that harmed the basic structure of the family and led to the abandonment of God and the "eat, drink, and be merry" attitude. In some

---

[1]   Chesler, *Politically Incorrect*, introduction.

ways, it is hard to overstate the role the world wars played, killing off roughly thirty-seven million people in the Great War, followed by an estimated eighty million in World War II. In addition to the great loss of life, there were also famines, disease, and massive destruction and annihilation of huge swaths of public and private property. This is the backdrop for the lives that emerged in the 1950s. Many people believe that those of us who reject feminism and all its empty promises merely want to return to the 1950s. It's true that the 1950s, unlike any decade since, at least made an effort to keep the veneer of life looking good as the Christian culture that had held society together for centuries began to wane. But the 1950s were no idyllic Camelot; they were simply the initial consequences of the great wars and the radical social upheaval and destruction they caused. This incubator of radical feminism is hardly a time to be coveted.

A brief look at the women who emerged as the goddesses of the Feminist Movement makes it clear that none of these women had a happy and carefree childhood. Gloria Steinem had a doting and loving father, but he was ever chasing the next get-rich-quick deal, leaving young Gloria as the caretaker of her bitter and mentally ill mother for many years. Meanwhile, Germaine Greer's attention-loving mother, while her husband was away fighting in the African theatre, entertained the troops in Australia. When the doting father returned from the war, the handsome man was so disfigured from battle and starvation that his family had a hard time finding him on the train platform. Germaine described her mom as "mean as cat piss" who would beat her, not often, but with passion, even though Germaine was a good child.

Germaine concluded that her unaffectionate mother simply didn't like her.

Phyllis Chesler has perhaps been the most outspoken about the resentment she held toward her own mother. "She criticized me constantly, yelled at me a lot, hit me sometimes and always threatened to turn me over to my father for more serious discipline."[2] Later in life, Chesler realized that her mother suffered from mental illness.

Betty Friedan and her mother would rage at each other. Her mother, a rare beauty who looked like she stepped out of a magazine, was frustrated with Betty, who seemed to work at being ugly. "I was very dominated by my mother. She was very critical of me and made me feel very insecure."[3] Betty hated her mother's phoniness, so she did the opposite, developing acerbic and rough ways of communicating with just about anyone.

A psychologist and author of seventeen books, Chesler seems to have dismissed a remarkable piece of evidence about feminism's source: the embattled relationship almost all of these women had with their parents, especially their mothers. These founders of feminism, whom Chesler dubs the Lost Girls, were women from broken homes who carried around deep mother wounds inflicted by little to no emotional support and physical affection. They matured physically, but somewhere on the inside they remained little girls. Their thirst to fill this gap was displayed in their rampant homosexuality and in their infantile effort to ignore the

---

2   Chesler, *Politically Incorrect*, loc. 141.
3   Marcia Cohen, *The Sisterhood* (Ballentine Books, 1988), 60.

problems they were creating through their "groundbreaking" behavior. "We are the women our parents warned us against, and we are proud," boasted Gloria Steinem. Yes, the era was full of sexual abuse and social inequalities, but their answer to fix them didn't help. "We picketed, marched, protested, sat in, and famously took over offices and buildings; helped women obtain illegal abortions; joined consciousness-raising groups; learned about orgasms; condemned incest, rape, sexual harassment, and domestic violence; organized speak-outs, crisis hotlines, and shelters for battered women; and came out as lesbians."[4]

The appearance of trying to help every woman who is treated unjustly provided much of the fuel to the cause. Who wouldn't want to help battered wives or a single mother who struggles to make ends meet? Their problem solving, however, through promiscuity, abortion, lesbianism, goddess worship, astrology charts, divorce, and drugs was like adding gas to the fire of these social problems. Because of their brokenness, as Chelser explains, they found it intoxicating: "Radical feminist ideas and activism were a bit like LSD. So many women became high at the same time that suddenly the world became psychedelically clear, and all the Lost Girls found ourselves and each other."[5]

The *sisterhood* bonded these outcasts together, linked by common mania, but also because they needed each other, particularly in the darker days before the matriarchy had any success. Gloria Steinem once said, "Any woman who

---

4   Chesler, *Politically Incorrect*, loc. 87.
5   Ibid.

chooses to behave like a full human being should be warned that the armies of the status quo will treat her as something of a dirty joke. . . . She will need her sisterhood."

More than just close friendships, the sisterhood became a place of proliferating lesbian relationships, a cabal to solidify the groupthink of the women's movement, and even operated like a coven because of the rampant witchcraft and goddess worship among members. Like everything else in the women's movement, these were not typical types of sisterly love and affection. "We were all lost in a dream—but we had never been so awake. Women who were once invisible to each other were now the only visible creatures," said Chesler. "Women—who used to see one another as wicked stepsisters—had magically transformed into fairy godmothers. . . . I was as foolish as only a young dreamer could be," she added, "I—but I was no longer alone; now there was a *we*—and *we* wanted to end the subjugation of women—now!"[6] Because of their broken relationships with their mothers and the radical break they made with any type of tradition—even first wave feminists—Chesler said that "psychologically, we second-wavers had no feminist foremothers and no biological mothers. We had only sisters."[7]

Kate Millett, High Priestess

In 1970, the academically successful but mentally unstable Kate Millett found herself on the cover of *Time* magazine with the title "The Politics of Sex: Kate Millett and Women's

---

6   Ibid., loc. 448.
7   Ibid., loc. 482.

Lib," featuring her book *Sexual Politics*. Considered ground-breaking, Millett quickly became the intellectual force behind radical feminism. *Time* called her the "high priest-ess" of the movement and her book, its bible. The *New York Times* also called her book "the Bible of Women's Liberation" and "a remarkable document because it analyzes the need and nature of sexual liberation while itself displaying the vir-tues of intellectual and emotional openness and lovingness."[8] *Time* also called her "the Karl Marx of the Women's Move-ment" because her book laid out a course in Marxism 101 for women. "Her thesis: The family is a den of slavery with the man as the Bourgeoisie and the woman and children as the Proletariat."

A few months after Millett appeared on *Time's* cover, the magazine ran a second article about her, this time less laudatory. The article, entitled "Women's Lib: A Second Look," attacked Millett for her bisexuality. The fame and the shame, many people say, destroyed her. Her personality wasn't strong enough for the glowing limelight, followed by the dark scrutiny.

"Kate had a s***load of charm and, in the beginning, a commanding presence," Phyllis Chesler recalls, "but she also had periods in which she didn't sleep, raged at others, attempted suicide, and exploited her groupies—all the while feeling victimized by them (which she was). She couldn't be counted on to remain lucid at a press conference. She also

---

8   Parul Sehgal and Neil Genzlinger, "Kate Millett, Groundbreaking Feminist Writer, Is Dead at 82," *The New York Times*, Septem-ber 6, 2017, https://www.nytimes.com/2017/09/06/obituaries/kate-millett-influential-feminist-writer-is-dead-at-82.html.

fell in love, and tried to have her way, quite aggressively, with woman after woman (including me)."[9]

Millett died in 2017, but her sister, Mallory Millett, has started speaking up about the irreparable damage Kate did to Western culture through the popularization of her dark and demented work. Mallory attests to the fact that Kate's mania wasn't brought on by the *Time* articles but had pre-existed her fame since childhood. "She was the most disturbed, megalomaniacal, evil and dishonest person I have ever known," Mallory said. "She tried to kill me so many times that it's now an enormous blur of traumatizing horrors. She was a sadist, a torturer, a deeply-engrained bully who took immense pleasure in hurting others."[10]

"What the *Time* article did do," Mallory says, "is it destroyed her marriage. Despite being seduced by a female professor in college, Kate had given up her lesbian lifestyle when she married Fumio Yoshimura, and for seventeen years, they had a happy marriage." After the *Time* article was published, Kate was ambushed at an evening church meeting by a cabal of lesbians at a church, who thought they were being left out of the movement's limelight. "To defend herself against their charges, Kate confessed that she had once been a lesbian, unaware that two *Time* reporters were among the throng. This was what prompted the second *Time* article, but it also led Kate back to promiscuity as a lesbian and the ruin of her life with Fumio. It was something that she would regret for the rest of her life."[11] Kate's relationship and

9   Chesler, *Politically Incorrect*, loc. 2939.
10   Mallory Millett, personal conversion with the author, spring 2018.
11   Ibid.

the years of heartache and regret it brought to both spouses was hardly an isolated case; the movement destroyed relationship after relationship with the promise of free love and liberation, where bodies were used for amusement, and vows and promises were quickly tossed aside.

Mallory, who spent a period devoted to her sister Kate and her radical ideas before returning to the Catholic faith of their childhood, eventually left Kate's inner circle when things just got too weird. But she spent enough time with women in the movement to see its underbelly. Mallory has dark stories that make it clear these women were clearly involved in the occult, with a Marxist twist.

"It was 1969 and she took me to a meeting at her friend, Lila Karp's place, in Greenwich Village," Mallory explains. "At a consciousness raising (an idea imported from Mao's China), twelve women gathered at a large table. They opened with a type of Litany from the Catholic Church . . . but, this time it was Marxism, the church of the Left."[12] This "litany" was chronicled in the introduction, but it's worth repeating:

> "Why are we here today?" the chairwoman asked.
>
> "To make revolution," they answered.
>
> "What kind of revolution?" she replied.
>
> "The Cultural Revolution," they chanted.
>
> "And how do we make Cultural Revolution?" she demanded.
>
> "By destroying the American family!" they answered.
>
> "How do we destroy the family?" she came back.

---

12   Millett, "Marxist Feminist's Ruined Lives."

"By destroying the American Patriarch," they cried exuberantly.

"And how do we destroy the American Patriarch?" she probed.

"By taking away his power!"

"How do we do that?"

"By destroying monogamy!" they shouted.

"How can we destroy monogamy?"

"By promoting promiscuity, eroticism, prostitution, abortion and homosexuality!" they resounded.[13]

Such antics might seem insignificant except for the fact that all of these goals have been achieved. The rhetoric used to convince women to engage in these things seems ridiculous now, but somehow it was compelling then.

The last straw for Mallory, when she knew she *had* to get away from Kate and her cronies, was when Kate aggressively tried to get Mallory to go to bed with her.

But the craziness didn't stop with Kate. "Shulamith Firestone called pregnancy 'barbaric,' preferred artificial reproduction and imagined a utopia in which children, like Eros, would roam freely throughout the world." Mallory adds, "Greer, with a PhD from Cambridge, encouraged women to taste their own menstrual blood and discouraged them from partnering monogamously. 'Women,' Greer claimed, 'have very little idea of how much men hate them.'"[14]

These ideas extended beyond their little troop of women through the women's studies programs they helped establish

---

13   Ibid.
14   Millett, personal conversation.

across the country. In those women's studies classes, a young impressionable girl, Mallory explains, "will be told, 'Be an outlaw, be a damned outlaw. . . . Every law was concocted by dead white men. Be a slut and be proud of it.'"[15] Millett and her crew of eleven young women lived by this very philosophy; they started calling themselves "sluts" and engaged in orgies and every other sort of thing that captured the imagination.

The most harrowing story in Mallory's memory is of a dinner party on Halloween night at Kate's loft apartment. Upon entering, there was a long, low table with twelve placements topped by a plate, a bowl of water, and sharp knife resting on it. In front of each place setting were twelve completely naked women, sitting cross legged on cushions. The naked woman at the head of the table was wrapped by a live ten-foot boa constrictor. Dumbstruck and appalled, Mallory and her friend watched in horror. They were invited to join in the ritual, but they told Kate they were just there to observe, which seemed to suit Kate since they were only willing to take off their shoes. "As they took their eyes off us to resume their ritual," Mallory explains, "we tiptoed to our shoes and crept out running down those flights like bats out of hell. My feet barely touched the steps until we burst out onto the Bowery, shaking and huffing in shock and terror."[16]

Mallory marvels at how it happened, how this anti-apostolic crowd succeeded so wildly in their ragtag efforts from start to finish. "How could twelve American women who were the most respectable types imaginable—clean

---

[15]   Ibid.
[16]   Ibid.

and privileged graduates of esteemed institutions: Colum-
bia, Radcliffe, Smith, Wellesley, Vassar—the uncle of one
was secretary of war under Franklin Roosevelt—plot such a
thing?" she asks. "Most had advanced degrees and appeared
cogent, bright, reasonable, and good. How did these girls
rationally believe they could succeed with such vicious gran-
diosity? And why?"[17] Clearly, there had to be more to their
motivation and Kate's mania. Their adherence to Marxism,
and their engagement in the occult, made it a perfect storm
of destruction; it was an anti-Marian bomb that is still
exploding throughout Western culture.

"I came to see all this lesbianism, witchcraft, atheistic politics as a psychotic dimension," Mallory said. "It is just plain
crazy to convince women that not only is it good to murder
your own child in your womb, but it's imperative that you
buck up and have the courage to do it. Their argument for
doing it was that men are killers so we must be like them.
We'll never see equality with men if we can't prove ourselves
capable of killing," she added. "There was a deadly concoc-
tion of their own twisted ideology along with the inflated
fears of the population explosion. These women were convinced they had to do it for the sake of their own future but
also to save our planet."[18]

Mallory says that Kate's friends were always covering for
her, getting her out of mental institutions and other tight
spots. Even after her death, they still covered up her radical
mental health issues while insisting on her genius, seen here

---

[17]   Ibid.
[18]   Ibid.

in this short eulogizing quote Gloria Steinem emailed to the *New York Times* after Kate's death:

> Kate was brilliant, deep, and uncompromising. She wrote about the politics of male dominance, of owning women's bodies as the means of reproduction, and made readers see this as basic to hierarchies of race and class. She was not just talking about unequal pay, but about woman-hatred in the highest places and among the most admired intellectuals. As Andrea Dworkin said, "The world was asleep, but Kate Millett woke it up."[19]

It was quite a rude awakening.

Free Love and the Lavender Menace

Men, as part of the patriarchy, were also the direct targets for radical feminists. They argued that men were the ones who had created the world wars, so men must be stopped—using any means possible, including sex-selective abortions to thin out their numbers. Fewer men meant less harm would afflict the planet. Men were the enemy. Therefore, monogamous heterosexual relationships were frowned upon while promiscuity of any stripe was lauded. With their elevated sense of the sisterhood, their own brokenness, and experience as Lost Girls, the highest ideal of feminism became lesbianism. A young Gloria Steinem wondered aloud when she, too, would finally be attracted to another woman. At some point,

---

[19] Sehgal and Genzlinger, "Kate Millet, Groundbreaking Feminist Writer, Is Dead at 82."

she and many other feminists like her made the transition from male lovers to lesbians. It was viewed as a rite of passage to wear the feminist badge. And instead of women jumping out of cakes for stag-parties, they engaged in their own forms of adult "entertainment," too sordid to mention here.

As an octogenarian, Steinem boasted that she had become gender neutral, as much female as she is male, or perhaps no gender at all. "In itself, homosexuality is as limiting as heterosexuality: the ideal should be to be capable of loving a woman or a man; either, a human being, without feeling fear, restraint, or obligation," wrote Simone de Beauvoir, apparently in a way that was compelling among these self-proclaimed misfits. "A gender-equal society would be one where the word 'gender' does not exist: where everyone can be themselves," said Steinem.

Kate Millett, oscillating between bisexuality and lesbianism at different stages of her life, weighed in on the important role homosexuality could play for the revolution. "A sexual revolution begins with the emancipation of women, who are the chief victims of patriarchy, and also with the ending of homosexual oppression." She didn't limit herself to adults, but thought intergenerational sex was important. She was sympathetic to abolishing the age of consent laws so that children could also express their sexuality, or have it expressed upon them. Millett added that "one of children's essential rights is to express themselves sexually, probably primarily with each other but with adults as well," and that "the sexual freedom of children is an important part of a sexual revolution. . . . If you don't change the social condition of children you still have an inescapable inequality."[20]

Cosmopolitan: Playboy for Playgirls

Helen Gurley Brown, Kate Millett's polar opposite personality-wise, has undoubtedly surpassed Kate's influence as founder of *Cosmopolitan* magazine. Gurley Brown, author of *Sex and the Single Girl*, was fascinated by the success of *Playboy* and decided to make her own version of it; she got pointers from Hugh Hefner and followed the *Playboy* model as closely as she could, right down to using the same writing agents and layout model. It quickly became the hottest women's magazine in the nation.[21] Revenues for the magazine went from $601,000 in 1964 to $47.7 million in 1985 (much of which came from advertising for the now $4 billion birth control industry). While others were struggling to get advertisers, *Cosmo* had no problem getting backers. Other magazines quickly followed the *Cosmo* model, to the point where there was very little difference between *Self, Glamour*, and *Cosmo* content.

Cosmo was all about selling a lifestyle. Motherhood was out, sex was in. Gurley Brown's motto was "Hard work and sex will set you free (as long as you don't have children)."[22] Even the throw pillow on a couch in the magazine's lobby said approvingly, "Good Girls Go to Heaven, Bad Girls Go

---

[20]   Hillary Frey, "Mother Courage. (Review)," *The Nation*, July 23, 2001, The Nation Institute.

[21]   Sue Ellen Browder, phone conversation, August 14, 2018.

[22]   Browder, *Subverted*, 35.

Everywhere."[23] As part of this lifestyle, a Cosmo Girl could be anything she wanted, except a "virgin or a mother." She could be a lesbian, a brothel owner, or a stripper, but she could not remain a virgin or become a mother. Cosmo Girls run roughshod over their fertility (although I'm sure this was never part of their advertising slogans). "Tough as a whore" was never meant to be a compliment, and yet the feminists turned it into just that.

Sue Ellen Browder, who started on staff and then free-lanced for Cosmopolitan for over two decades, was a dutiful writer of fiction for the popular magazine. Most readers didn't realize, however, that she was making stories up. "Many of the alleged 'real people' we wrote about in the magazine were entirely fictitious. . . . The Cosmo Girl was not a real person but a persona, a mask the single girl lonely and alone in the world could put on to turn herself into the object of a man's sexual fantasies."[24] The typical Cosmo Girl "had a glamour job, traveled a lot, and spent her hard-earned cash on pricey commodities to support her self-entered lifestyle."[25] "Make no mistake," Browder is quick to add, "we're not talking here about what's popularly called *spin*. This was hard-core sex-revolution propaganda masquerading as fluff."[26]

Browder eventually converted to Catholicism, but that was after the damage was done as a *Cosmo* writer. She makes it clear that they weren't doing women (or men) any favors, despite appearances. "As we visibly pretended to set women

---

[23]   Ibid., 38.
[24]   Ibid., 37.
[25]   Ibid., 39.
[26]   Ibid., 40.

sexually free from their biology (via the pill and abortion), we were invisibly catering to and even helping to create, millions of sexually troubled, insecure, confused women, who were likely to attract equally confused, insecure men."[27]

Gurley Brown's influence didn't end with the magazine. In 1986, the magazine mogul invited the editors from thirteen different magazines—including *Good Housekeeping*, *Redbook*, *Harper's*, *Elle*, *Savvy*, *Family Circle, and others—to a meeting*. "Helen spoke at the meeting," Browder explains, "and the editors agreed to run pro-abortion articles in their March 1987 issues. Among the articles that appeared in *Cosmopolitan* that month were: 'Abortion: Your Right Under Attack,' 'Choice: Separating Myth from Fact,' 'My Illegal Abortion,' and an article on why eight famous women were pro-choice."[28] *These women colluded* in promoting pro-choice articles to soften American women to abortion.

Magazines, starting with *Cosmo* and all the others following suit, were the sales arm of Kate Millett's "litany." It was Gurley Brown and her minions that were selling the American public on "promiscuity, eroticism, prostitution, abortion and homosexuality," while laughing all the way to the bank.

Wounds that Won't Heal

At the end of her book, Phyllis Chesler lists the many feminists for whom she still holds great affection, even though

---

27   Ibid., 40.
28   Sue Ellen Browder, "Magazines Like Teen Vogue Hard Sell Abortion to Fill the Pockets of Big Companies," *The Federalist*, February 28, 2017, http://thefederalist.com/2017/02/28/magazines-like-teen-vogue-hard-sell-abortion-fill-pockets-big-companies/.

they have passed on; women such as Kate Millett, Andrea Dworkin, Rivka Haut, and Jill Johnston. Chesler worked with many other women, scores of whom didn't make the list because they betrayed her and the sisterhood at some point. The other striking thing about Chesler's close cadre of sisterhood friends was how many of them had severe mental health issues. "I realized that just as I was once afraid to admit—even to myself—that mental illness plagued my high-functioning mother and members of my family, so too have I denied the extent to which many of the most charismatic and original of feminist thinkers were mentally ill," she wrote. "I don't mean neurotic, difficult, anxious, or eccentric. I mean clinically schizophrenic or manic depressive, suicidal, addicted to drugs or alcohol, or afflicted with a personality disorder."[29]

It is not clear if any of these women finally came to terms with their mothers and found the healing they needed from their deep wounds. One of the tough realities of parental wounds is that the child, who loves the parent despite deep hurt, doesn't want to go to that place of accusing the parent of terrible things. George MacDonald, who believed that Christ could redeem even Lilith, spoke to this reality in his book *Lilith: A Romance*. At one point in the novel, Lona— the daughter of Lilith and Adam—and her community are forced to fight Lilith's aggressive and murderous village. Before the battle, Lona, speaking about her mother, says, "I would give my life to have my mother! She might kill me

---

29   Chesler, *Politically Incorrect*, loc. 2129.

if she liked! I should just kiss her and die!"[30] It is the static nature of a child to love her mother, no matter what. In fact, it isn't hard to imagine the aborted children offering these sentiments to the mothers that will never hold them. Read it again: "I would give my life to have my mother! She might kill me if she liked! I should just kiss her and die!"

The Lost Girls, these girls who were never affirmed properly by their parents, who looked under every rock and in every dark place for the answers to their questions—to affirm their lives, bring them peace, and flourish as authentic women—are the ones who have shaped the large majority of our cultural dialogue. Ultimately, their search has been fruitless. "Fruitless" not because they didn't achieve their goals—the demonic desires chanted by Kate Millett and her anti-apostles have been realized through their victorious cultural revolution—but because it has only been destructive and debasing, not constructive and elevating. They destroyed the family out of hostility. As Fr. George Rutler says, "Hostility to truth is nurtured by the love of lies," and the lies of the matriarchy sound empowering and liberating. The matriarchy sought to make the world a more comfortable place by unleashing the sensual above the rational and tolerance over principle, but at a terrible cost to everyone.

Our world has become an orphanage, which is what happens when we get rid of the cross and "the Woman who stood by it."[31]

---

30 George MacDonald, *Lilith: A Romance*, Kindle Edition.

31 Fr. George Rutler, *The Seven Wonders of the Ancient World* (San Francisco: Ignatius Press, 1998), 68.

Chapter 6

The New Matriarchy: Fashionable Dictators

"I think that testosterone is a rare poison."

—Germaine Greer

It's no secret that women tend to look to other women for ideas. We applaud this in the multi-billion-dollar fashion industry and entrust most of our wardrobe and fashion choices to whatever is trending. In the movie *The Devil Wears Prada*, fashion mogul Miranda Priestly (Meryl Streep) breaks in her idealistic new assistant Andy Sachs (Anne Hathaway), who dreams of doing something more important than matching skirts with sweaters. When Miranda catches Andy smirking at serious chatter over denim skirts, Miranda unloads: "See that droopy sweater you're wearing? That blue was on a dress Cameron Diaz wore on the cover of Runway—shredded chiffon by James Holt. The same blue quickly appeared in eight other designers' collections and eventually made its way to the secondary designers, the department store labels, and then to some lovely Gap Outlet, where you no doubt found it. That color is worth millions of dollars and many jobs."[1]

We women appreciate that others work hard to provide us new selections every season. What we may not realize, however, is that the marketplace of ideas works like the fashion industry. Instead of elite designers, the political and social elite—the matriarchy who are beholden to anti-Marian ideas—provide the parameters about what we think. Instead of skirt lengths and eye-shadow hues, they suggest intellectual trends that we scarcely know are being dictated to us through every possible avenue, from women's magazines to popular daytime television and, especially, mainstream media.

What is not well-known is that these layers of influence have also bled into the world of ideas through the media and cultural celebrities, such as Hillary Clinton, Gloria Steinem, and Maureen Dowd. Ideas pitched by these elite women trickle down into the daily lives of millions of women across the country and around the world through programs such as Rachel Maddow or *The View*, and then into sitcoms, such as Lena Dunham's *Girls*. Notions like *women can only be free if they are able to abort their children, gender is a fluid thing* (unless one wants to become heterosexual), *masculinity is toxic*, or *women must become the same as men* all started with elite women and are piped into our lives like elevator music.

---

[1] "The Devil Wears Prada," screenplay, http://www.dailyscript.com/scripts/devil_wears_prada.pdf.

This shrill female chorus has its hands in every cultural pot. Look at New York, the heart of big media, which largely controls the news narrative. Most smaller news sources rely upon the *New York Times*, the *Associated Press*, and the major television networks. New York also has the fashion industry, which has blurred the lines between clothing us and scolding us about how we are to think on any given topic. Pouty and emaciated women say more with their aloof sophistication when coupled with a political idea than any series of books ever could.

These ideas have also been chiseled into public policy in Washington, DC, where there are plenty of politicians beholden to Planned Parenthood. *The Washington Post* also holds significant national and international sway. In politics and media alike, there are a lot of platitudes and impassioned cries to fight for all women, just so long as we are talking about the right women (and not those waiting to be born). Comments like former secretary of state Madeleine Albright's that "there's a special place in Hell for women who don't help each other" are subtle ways of virtue signaling how all women should think, or more importantly, vote. Meanwhile, female politicians and lobbyists, aided by journalists and celebrities, hold the strings of most every political issue by their votes, rulings, and lobbying for political causes, often offering access to campaign cash, or the promise of political pork for their districts. Dr. Jennifer Roback Morse and law professor Helen Alvaré have both chronicled the sad role that public policy and legislation have played in perpetuating the myths of the sexual revolution by giving sexual activity and preferences legal priority over the needs of children and families.[2]

Skipping over "flyover" country, we move to Hollywood and the music industry, which work hand-in-hand to further the message that sexual license of any stripe is fun, liberating, and free of consequences. Some of Hollywood's underbelly has recently been revealed, showing (a) that some men are benefiting immensely from the matriarchal narrative (Harvey Weinstein was a huge Planned Parenthood donor), and (b) that the myth of sisterhood among liberal women extends only so far when male bosses are calling the shots. It seems there were plenty of women who were aware of what was going on behind closed hotel doors but said nothing until their reputations were at stake.

And then there is the matriarchy's publishing arm—*Cosmopolitan, Marie Claire, People, Vogue*, and so on—that reach women at the checkout stand. These magazines have become toxic blends of celebrity worship, virtue signaling about politics, the occult, and old-fashioned gossip. Though appearing benign and frivolous, magazines no longer have a line between editorial content and advertising. The two spoons full of sugar in their savvy and seductive images have helped women swallow even the most unsavory of ideas. As Myrna Blyth explains, using storytelling and carefully selected headlines, magazines have capitalized upon the idea that women are victims. Women who are victims are much

---

[2]   Helen Alvaré, *Putting Children's Interests First in US Family Law and Policy: With Power Comes Responsibility* (Cambridge University Press, 2017) and Jennifer Roback Morse, *The Sexual State* (Charlotte: TAN Books, 2018).

more likely to keep purchasing content that underscores their victimhood while also offering suggestions on how to resolve it. It started with "Dear Abby" but has proliferated into a monstrous monopoly of begetting victimhood to every woman, no matter what her circumstances, simply because she is a woman.

Universities, with a few notable exceptions, are also doing the bulk of the heavy lifting to promote the matriarchy's vision. Women's studies departments, many of them established by Kate Millett and her contemporaries, are awash in ideology. The intellectual poison scarcely remains there, broadly infecting other academic departments as well. Margaret, a recent graduate of Harvard, recounts several incidents at her *alma mater* that make it clear the professors there are willingly manipulating rhetoric to reach their own ends.[3] During a small meeting with one hundred female student actvists, professors, and students, someone asked what the future of abortion promotion is. The honored guest, Frances Kissling, responded, "Now that there are ultrasounds, everyone knows it is a baby. We need another strategy." No one in the audience seemed to bat an eye at the notion feminists had to figure out another way to justify killing children. Margaret also experienced professors like Elizabeth Schüssler Fiorenza and Mark Jordan, who advocate for selling the public on extreme ideas with the hope that it normalizes the less extreme, such as gay marriage and pederasty. They believe

---

3   "Margaret" is a pseudonym. Private conversation with the author, November, 2018.

that truth is a spectrum and their goal is to pull people closer to their cause by pushing the boundaries beyond it.

So why do women fall into the trap of following this line of thinking? Partially because women have been hardwired to consider what other women think and how they act and then to mimic it. It is part of our set of survival skills. More significantly, the matriarchy acts as a kind of gatekeeper, preventing different voices from being heard in the public square. And finally, because it is so ubiquitous, most women assume that this is the right route to happiness; surely all these experts must be right about relationships, culture, human sexuality, and careers. But never addressed is the disconnect between what the matriarchy presents and what actually brings happiness. We don't hear about the broken woman after an abortion, the career woman who wishes she had more children (or any children at all), the extensive physical damage caused by the pill, or the children devastated by divorce. And yet, this is the wreckage left behind by the culture the matriarchy has produced. On the other side of the coin, we also don't hear about peaceful and joy-filled religious sisters who have given their lives for Christ, or very contented mothers of big families who wouldn't trade their "jobs" for the world.

Nevertheless, because of its sense of sisterhood and commitment to "girl power," feminism is the badge carried by nearly every modern-day woman who considers herself liberated, self-determining, and independent. Feminism has effectively made itself fashionable and painted its enemies as awkward, tired, and out of touch zombies, like Stepford Wives—so much so that few American women today can articulate any sort of alternative to the trendy positions repeated in political slogans on *The View* or in *Cosmo.*

Women have been duped into thinking that this *is* the only way that modern women can think.

Newspeak

Like the fashion industry, fashionable ideas start with influencers, such as a statement by Hillary, Alyssa Milano, Tina Fey, or Chelsea Handler, followed by a well-placed message in *Girls*, then picked up by pundits on MSNBC, and finally trickling down to emotional appeals on *The View* or in *Cosmo*, and so on. Like Andy's blue sweater, thousands of people helped craft and perpetuate these messages. These are the ideas presented as acceptable for public consumption. The influence is so subtle yet so pervasive that even having a discussion on this topic can be difficult because we live under the impression that we are free thinkers; the irony is that thinkers are generally *not* free when they think just like everybody else.

So what are the current thought trends? The current crop of "acceptable" tenets include:

- Women are always victims.
- Men and masculinity must change.
- Others must provide women unrestricted access to contraception and abortion.
- Women will only be equal when they are considered *exactly* the same as men and, therefore, must be granted special safeguards from and privileges over men (again, we never said it was logical).

- Society must accept gender neutrality and fluidity (unless it flows back to heterosexuality).
- Men have nothing to say about abortion since they don't have a uterus (unless they are transgender— then they can say whatever they want as long as it is in favor of abortion).
- And the newest one: Let's share our lady-parts! Grab your pink hat or your vagina dress.

These basic ideas have become the very air of public discourse. When any are violated, matriarchs are quick to remind everyone that women are victims and throw a collective tantrum. And whenever an elite woman is honored for being brave and courageous, she is almost without fail doing so within the comfortable boundaries set by the matriarchy.

Women who espouse these ideas are presented as savvy, sophisticated, important, well-spoken, right thinking, free thinkers. On the other hand, women who oppose these ideas are branded as frumpy, fundamentalist, wrong-thinking, unhip, and kowtowers to the backward way things have always been.

Lest you think it an exaggeration, consider well-known women who don't ascribe to the matriarchy. There are about five that might come to mind, none of whom the media treats well. Discussion is hermetically-sealed so no one notices that there might be another way to think, which is how Academy Award winning actress Natalie Portman only recently discovered, much to her surprise, that there is actually a case against abortion. Woman who operate outside these parameters are labeled "problematic" or non-women.

The sisterhood only extends to like-minded women (read: abortion supporters), and women who fall outside of the groupthink are really somehow not women. As we saw in the last chapter, women can be psychotic, schizophrenic, addicts, lesbians, or anything else under the sun, but virgins, contented mothers, and pro-lifers are no longer considered women. These non-women are immediately assailed with *ad hominem* attacks and words put in their mouths, suggesting that women should be doormats or slaves, even if this isn't at all what they say or think. There is no happy medium of thought or leaving the safe intellectual confines of the matriarchy. Kate Millett once said, "Many women do not recognize themselves as discriminated against; no better proof could be found of the totality of their conditioning." The non-woman's problem is that she can't even see the reality of her plight. "Real" women, however, see their plight and in order to show just how liberated they are from it, they "shout their abortion." A new website touting this freedom features articles on the topic entitled "My Abortion Was Gentle, Irreverent, and Empowering," "Best Decision of My Life," "Abortion Is Mercy," and "Thank God for Abortion."

Again, there is a pattern here that goes beyond just women behaving badly. It is tied closely to Marxist thought. Ryzard Legutko, commenting on the ideological connections between the Soviet proletariat and feminism, outlines the parallels of what happens when the old communal bonds, such as the family and the Church, have been tossed aside. Something must fill the gap: "The feminist ideology, for example, proclaimed that women are united by a special feeling of togetherness and solidarity, which they, unsurprisingly, called a bond of sisterhood. It does not require much perceptiveness to see that the women thus defined were a close equivalent of Marx's proletariat. Like the proletariat, the women-sisters were believed to form an international or rather transnational political group whose primary reason of being is empowerment of their entire sex and liberation of all possible chains imposed on them by history and by men."[4]

Just like the proletariat, the generic word *women*, Legutko explains, "is an abstract concept that does not denote any actual existing community, but only an imagined collective made an object of political worship among feminist organizations and their allies."[5] He continues:

> But the paradox is that this feminist woman, being a figment of political imagination, is considered by feminists to be a proper woman, a woman in a strict sense, the truest woman, just as for the communists the Marxist proletariat was the truest representative of the working class. By the same token a real woman living in a real society, like a real worker living in a real society, is politically not to be trusted because she deviates too much from the political model. In fact, a non-feminist woman is not a woman at all, just as a noncommunist worker is not really a proletarian.[6]

---

4 Legutko, *The Demon in Democracy*, 94.
5 Ibid.
6 Ibid.

The non-woman, therefore, must be denied a voice so that she cannot do damage to the ideological bulwark holding up the effort.

More than Feminism

One of the strangleholds that feminism has had upon women is the impression it offers that women could do nothing before its arrival and that it is the only movement that has been of assistance to women—both of which are patently false. Kate O'Beirne writes, "Long before NOW held its first organizational meeting, there were female role models who exemplified initiative, intelligence, and independence." She adds, "America's first large network of professional women was Catholic nuns. In the 1900s, they built and ran the country's largest private school and hospital systems. These women were nurses, teachers—and CEOs."[7]

Assisting others, living in deep charity for those in need, caring for the poor, the sick, the aged, are gifts brought to the world through Christianity. Because charity isn't a tenant of other faiths, charitable and educational institutes haven't arisen with them. Rarely do we see Islamic hospitals or Buddhist adoption agencies. They might exist in the singular, but they are not the specific fruit of these religions. Hospitals, universities, grammar and high schools, these were part and parcel of the Catholic ethos and carried out on a large scale by female religious, who handled them with grace and professionalism.

---

7   O'Beirne, *Women Who Make the World Worse*, xix.

Contrast this with the abortion industry that has been caught red-handed lying about offering mammograms to clients (they have no mammogram machines) and selling fetal parts to outside vendors for large financial kickbacks and without the permission of the mothers.

No Room for Logic and Truth

The pervasiveness of the matriarchy's narrative keeps us from looking deeper into the underpinnings of its arguments, so much so that most don't recognize they are largely divorced from logic, science, and basic common sense. Here is where the fingerprints of the goddess movement and its adherence to intuition, emotion, and invention are most on display. Truly, the empress has no clothes, but we have spent decades commenting on her fine raiment, color, and style so that almost no one dares comment on her intellectual nudity.

Many of us have experienced the feeling that feminists are intransigent on so many ideas, even when the science directly opposes their arguments, but this is the crux of why. Like we already saw, radical feminism is an enslaving attitude that they have sunk their faith into; it is a perfect new dogma that must be defended at all costs, even the cost of complete surreality. Instead of saying, "We were wrong about how much kids need parents or about when life begins," they dig their heels in deeper, saying they just need more sex, government programs, or better education. Anything but the family. Anything but life.

After looking further, it seems clear that the deeper currents of thought in feminist philosophy are completely absent in the public national debates. When talking about women's issues, feminists aren't searching for truth but pushing savvy talking points; they aren't seeking authentic justice but maintaining a shallow narrative; and they aren't promoting real love for womanhood but furthering a distorted agenda. Ultimately, feminism and its goals appear to be built upon trends, fads, emotional whims, and political posturing that are all tethered to the dogma of abortion. No longer a compelling philosophy, it is simply another big business, where billions are made, careers are built for power and prestige, and women sipping chardonnay over salads glibly make decisions that will affect thousands and thousands of lives (and deaths). As Gloria Steinem said, "Logic is in the eye of the logician."

The feminist movement hasn't always been a hollow shell. Once upon a time, it was founded upon principles of justice and truth. It appears, however, that the feminists of the '60s discovered that logic and tight reasoning are nothing compared to the power of images and sound bites; for example, wire hangers, GI Jane Fonda, and pink sneakers seem to say it all, while catch-phrases like *pro-choice, war on women*, and *rare, safe, and legal* stymie any rational debate about what is truly good for American women.

Ironically, for a movement originally trying to dispel the belief that women are not the intellectual equals of men and are too emotional, much of the feminist rhetoric is simply that: spewed emotions. Even feminist Camille Paglia has been critical. "The headlong rush to judgment by so many well-educated, middle-class women in the #MeToo movement has been startling and dismaying," she said in a recent interview. "Their elevation of emotion and group solidarity over fact and logic has resurrected damaging stereotypes of women's irrationality that were once used to deny us the vote."[8] Any of the intellectual pillars that once held feminism aloft have been reduced to arguments based on emotions, bullying, mockery, or childish tantrums. Modern feminists unconsciously embody the old misogynistic stereotypes that early feminists fought to refute.

The Future Is Female?

One of the pithy slogans, that we saw back in chapter 4, to come out of Hilary Clinton's presidential campaign was "The future is female." As the *Washington Post* reported, Clinton recycled this phrase from a couple of lesbians from the 1970s. Liza Cowan snapped a photo of her then-girlfriend Alix Dobkin sporting the phrase on a t-shirt, publishing it as part of a slide show, "What the Well Dressed Dyke Will Wear." Explaining how the slogan came about, Cowan said, "If we are to have a future, it must be female, because the rule of men—patriarchy—has just about devastated life on this beautiful little planet. The essence and the spirit of the future must be female. So the phrase becomes not just a slogan, but a spell. For the good of all."[9]

8   Claire Lehmann, "Camille Paglia: It's Time for a New Gender Map of the World," *Quillette*, November 10, 2018, https://quillette.com/2018/11/10/camille-paglia-its-time-for-a-new-map-of-the-gender-world/.

9   Katie Mettler, "Hillary Clinton just said it, but 'the future is female' began as a 1970s lesbian separatist slogan," *The Washington Post*, February 8, 2017, https://www.washingtonpost.com/news/morning-mix/wp/2017/02/08/hillary-clinton-just-said-it-

What Cowan makes clear in her now-famous slogan is that she, too, has bought into a myth about the women's movement, that if women were to rule the world, peace, harmony, and love would be the natural result. As author Leland Lewis wrote, "If women governed the entire world, it is my theory that soon we would have world peace and healing of the entire planet."[10] Actor Mark Hamill, who plays Luke Skywalker in the Star Wars franchise, recently tweeted this on the topic: "For centuries, men have had their chance to rule government with middling-to-poor results. Who's ready to let women take charge completely? Just women. I know I am."[11]

While it sounds lovely, the reality is that there is very little evidence this sort of utopia could happen when women are in charge. If we just look at the women's movement itself, Phyllis Chesler makes it very clear that the movement was not led by saintly women; back stabbing, intellectual theft, jealousy, envy, and pettiness were part and parcel of the feminist experience. "Women did not always treat each other kindly," Chesler explains. "Somehow we expected feminists, who are also women, to behave in radically different ways. We were shocked as we learned one by one, that feminists didn't always treat each other with respect or compassion."[12] She adds, "Like most women, feminists engaged in smear

---

but-the-future-is-female-began-as-a-1970s-lesbian-separatist-slo-gan/?noredirect=on.

[10] Sri Leland Lewis, *Random Molecular Mirroring* (self-pub., 2002). (I found this quote online. The book is available on Kindle, but I can't bring myself to purchase it.)

[11] Mark Hamill (@HamillHimself), Twitter, November 13, 2018.

[12] Chesler, *Politically Incorrect*, loc. 464.

and ostracism campaigns against any woman with whom they disagreed, whom they envied, or who was different in some way."[13] As a trained psychologist, Chesler admits, "Only now, half a century later, do I understand that women in groups tend to demand uniformity, conformity, shoulder-to-shoulder nonhierarchical sisterhood—one in which no one is more rewarded than anyone else. Marxism and female psychology are a natural fit psychologically."[14] What Chesler finally discovered is that women generally have a very different approach to the world, which is something we saw in chapter 2; it is not hierarchical, like the military, Church hierarchy, or royalty, but is meant to be egalitarian, where all women are to remain on the same level, and those who rise above the others must be brought back down into conformity. Like communism before it, its adherents would rather see their whole enterprise destroy itself than to see others succeed.

Up until now, the ramifications that the matriarchy has had upon men has not been discussed, but the evidence is more than significant that men have not flourished under the current matriarchal monopoly. The open vilification of men, of testosterone, of "toxic masculinity," has left men not knowing their place. Explaining the problem, Bishop Robert Barron said, "In the midst of a 'you-go-girl' feminist culture, many boys and young men feel adrift, afraid that any expression of their own good qualities will be construed as aggressive or insensitive."[15] The auxiliary bishop of Los

---

13   Ibid.
14   Ibid., loc. 500.
15   Robert Barron, "The Trouble with the 'You Go Girl,' Culture,"

Angeles calls the now ubiquitous avenging woman of our culture the "all conquering female." This type of woman is portrayed over and over again in the media, as Bishop Barron explains, "Almost without exception, she is under-estimated by men and then proves herself more intelligent, cleverer, more courageous, and more skilled than any man. Whether we're talking about a romantic comedy, an office-drama, or an adventure movie, the all conquering female will almost inevitably show up. And she *has* to show her worth in a domineering way, that is to say, over and against the men. For her to appear strong, they have to appear weak."[16]

The "all conquering female" is not just in movies but everywhere—commercials, novels, soap operas, music vid-eos—while male virtues are trampled upon. In the book *The Great Mother*, psychologist Erich Neumann says, "Matriar-chal womanhood assumes a character of the 'terrible' in its relation to the males."[17] That is, the power and position that women are given when they are put in charge, unless tem-pered by virtue, most often leads to maltreatment of men by rendering them useless. Like we saw in chapter 2, because of women's built-in vulnerability, without virtue they will nat-urally gravitate toward the vices of jealousy and envy, which will not allow others to flourish.

Beyond Neumann's extensive research, other matriar-chies have been scrutinized with similar results: take away men's responsibility to lead, protect, and care for the general

---

Word on Fire, October 18, 2016, https://www.wordonfire.org/resources/article/the-trouble-with-the-you-go-girl-culture/5291/.

[16] Ibid.

[17] Neumann, *Great Mother*, 267.

welfare of his people or family, and he ends up unfocused, without a mission, and adrift in life. Keith Pariot, a member of the matriarchal Indian state of Meghalaya, speaks of the kind of demoralization that happens to him and other men in the tribe. In his language, "[a] tree is masculine, but when it is turned into wood, it becomes feminine. The same is true of many of the nouns in our language. When something becomes useful, its gender becomes female."[18] What happens to the men, he adds, is that "matriliny breeds a culture of men who feel useless."[19] In another matriliny tribe in China, "Men are little more than studs, sperm donors who insem- inate women but have, more often than not, little involve- ment in their children's upbringing.[20]

It is arguable that, because of feminism, we live in an unrecognized matriliny, where the current matriarchy is doing what they always do: setting men adrift, unmoor- ing them from authentic responsibility, a sense of purpose, and a mission. As author Joseph Pearce wrote, "The truth is that the healthiest societies are always in one important sense matriarchies. They are societies in which strong and virtuous women raise strong and virtuous children, and in which well-behaved wives rein in the unruly passions of their poorly-behaved husbands. The unhealthiest societies

---

[18]   Timothy Allen, "Meghalaya, India: Where women rule, and men are suffragettes," *BBC News*, January 19, 2012, https://www.bbc. com/news/magazine-16592633.

[19]   Ibid.

[20]   Hannah Booth, "The Kingdom of Women," *The Guardian*, April 1, 2017,https://www.theguardian.com/lifeandstyle/2017/apr/01/ the-kingdom-of-women-the-tibetan-tribe-where-a-man-is-never- the-boss.

are patriarchies in which the power of men runs riot because the power of well-behaved women to restrain them has been weakened. The most unhealthy society of all is one in which the women want to run riot with the men."[21] It seems clear that not only are we living in a society where the women want to run riot with the men but even one step further, where the women want to run everything.

The Kavanaugh Crucible

The confirmation hearings of Supreme Court justice Brett Kavanaugh in 2018 was hugely revelatory of the typical tactics used by the matriarchy to get its way. All of the theatrics, every anti-Marian tactic, was summoned because of the concern that their "sacrament"—abortion—could be on the chopping block.

Despite the lack of evidence against him beyond one woman's testimony that went uncorroborated by any of the other witnesses present, Kavanaugh was subject to terrible abuse.[22] Beyond the accusations, his character was first under attack because he was too outspoken, too forthright, too strong in his opinions as he defended himself against evidence-less accusations. He then received further scorn when his eyes

---

21 Joseph Pearce, "The Wisdom and Wickedness of Women," *The Imaginative Conservative*, April 19, 2015, http://www.theimaginativeconservative.org/2015/04/the-wisdom-and-wickedness-of-women.html.

22 The Senate Judiciary Committee has since released a 414-page summary concluding that there was no evidence to support allegations against Kavanaugh, Nov. 3, 2018, https://www.judiciary.senate.gov/press/rep/releases/senate-judiciary-committee-releases-summary-of-investigation-from-supreme-court-confirmation.

welled up with tears as Senator Lindsey Graham spoke about Kavanaugh's daughter praying for the very woman who was trying to destroy his life. There is no satisfying the insatiable.

In response to the Kavanaugh hearing, retired history professor Victoria Bissell Brown published news of her rant toward men in the *Washington Post* in an article entitled "Thanks for not raping us, all you 'good men.' But it's not enough." "I yelled at my husband last night. Not pick-up-your-socks yell. Not how-could-you-ignore-that-red-light yell. This was real yelling. This was 30 minutes of from-the-gut yelling," Bissell Brown explains. "I blew. Hard and fast. And it terrified me. I'm still terrified by what I felt and what I said. . . . In that roiling moment, screaming at my husband as if he represented every clueless male on the planet (and I every angry woman of 2018), I announced that I hate all men and wish all men were dead."[23] The angry seventy-year-old grandmother continued:

> I said the meanest thing I've ever said to him: Don't you dare sit there and sympathetically promise to change. Don't say you will stop yourself before you blurt out some impatient, annoyed, controlling remark. No, I said, you can't change. You are unable to change. You don't have the skills and you won't do it. You, I said, are one of the good men. You respect women, you believe in women, you like women, you

---

23   Victoria Bissell Brown, "Thanks for not raping us, all you 'good men.' But it's not enough." *The Washington Post*, Oct. 12, 2018. https://www.washingtonpost.com/outlook/2018/10/12/thanks-not-raping-us-all-you-good-men-its-not-enough/?noredirect=on&utm_term=.943f0f3f7c1c

don't hit women or rape women or in any way abuse women. You have applauded and funded feminism for a half-century. You are one of the good men. And you cannot change. You can listen all you want, but that will not create one iota of change.[24]

Bissell Brown spewed her vitriol at her shocked and hurt husband because he and other men hadn't gotten together to change the world like feminists had. Because men didn't act like women. For decades, women have been asking men to listen to them while simultaneously telling them to shut up (they don't know anything about women or victimhood). One can almost hear echoes of Eve screaming at Adam as they leave the garden, "Why didn't you do something?"

Ironically, in the end, Bissell Brown laments that there is no longer the patriarch, Noah, ready to help us combat the flood of memories that she claims every woman is drowning in (remember, we are all victims), "Pay attention people: If we do not raise boys to walk humbly and care deeply, if we do not demand that men do more than just listen, we will all drown in the flood. And there is no patriarchal Noah to save us."[25]

Peggy Noonan also chimed in on the histrionics provoked by the confirmation hearings:

The howling and screeching that interrupted the hearings and the voting, the people who clawed on the door of the court, the ones who chased senators

---

24   Ibid.
25   Ibid.

through the halls and screamed at them in elevators, who surrounded and harassed one at dinner with his wife, who disrupted and brought an air of chaos, who attempted to thwart democratic processes so that the people could not listen and make their judgments:

Do you know how that sounded to normal people, Republican and Democratic and unaffiliated? It sounded demonic. It didn't sound like "the resistance" or #MeToo. It sounded like the shrieking in the background of an old audiotape of an exorcism.[26]

All of these theatrics were yet again fueled by an irrational rage, unhinged from reason and civility. And when it seemed women couldn't go lower, their next response was predictable: witches rallied together and put hexes upon him. The witches said, "We will be embracing witchcraft's true roots as the magik [sic] of the poor, the downtrodden and disenfranchised and it's[sic] history as often the only weapon, the only means of exacting justice available to those of us who have been wronged by men just like him."[27]

26   Peggy Noonan, "Voices of Reason – And Unreason," *The Wall Street Journal*, October 11, 2018, https://www.wsj.com/articles/voices-of-reasonand-unreason-1539299053.

27   Heather Dockray, "Witches Plan Multiple Mass Hexes of Supreme Court Justice Brett Kavanaugh," *Mashable*, October 17, 2018, https://mashable.com/article/witches-hex-kavanaugh/#Ke WeUYGPqsqr.

Why Don't Men Fight Back?

Why is it, then, that men don't fight back and defend themselves better against the matriarchy? There are four basic reasons: First, by and large, men are simply at a loss as to how to combat this scourge on the culture without seemingly adding to the problem—of appearing sexist, or somehow trying to undo the advances that women have been able to make over the last five decades. They love women and don't want to rock the boat that the majority of women have boarded, especially if they are going to be targeted in such a way that will undermine their relationships, income, or social status.

Second, fighting women goes against men's better nature. Men in Western cultures are generally not comfortable with the idea of hitting or verbally attacking women (yes, domestic violence is sadly a different thing). From their earliest days, boys have an innate desire to fight the bad guys. Even boys given dolls to play with will use the dolls as makeshift guns. Soldiering comes naturally to them. But women aren't supposed to be the enemy. It shouldn't surprise us that even Adam (before the fall!) was more inclined just to eat the fruit than to fight with Eve.

Third, feminism satisfies men's baser instincts. Men on the more predatory scale consider themselves beneficiaries of feminism, which allows them to have shallow and frequent hook-ups whenever they fancy, particularly with social media apps like Tinder.

And finally, the sexual revolution has provided them with a way out of dealing with women altogether. Porn saps the spirit and the outrage of many a man, leaving him satisfied and spent, such that he isn't much motivated to react or even to engage women. The rise in sexbots allow men to sidestep them entirely.

The tactics invoked by anti-Marian women, tantrums and bullying, have done much to simultaneously keep men in check while also creating a deep poison and division between the sexes. Both are marks of the fallen angel who wants to destroy the natural icon of God found in men and women living in harmony with one another. This raises the likelihood that there is something significant for women concerning the complementarity of men: maybe women *need* men to balance them out, to reign in their inclinations to insatiability, irrationality, and envy. Perhaps the "all conquering female" doesn't know when to quit, except when she has truly conquered everything, totally demolishing it and grinding it into a powder (to borrow a phrase from Lenin). Perhaps it is this dominant political posturing of women, unhinged from rationality and civility, that has led us once again to the "terrible mother" type of culture?

The matriarchy has been incredibly successful in making over women to be the whores, dykes, and bitches they envisioned. Ironically, they also show us daily how miserable they are in their debased state. The girl of our day "has degraded herself from an archetypical princess, whose beauty was both a challenge and a prize for a young man, to a beggar that hopes that the man she is living with and to whom she is trying to prove she can be a good wife will eventually marry her," said cultural commentator Barbara Dafoe Whitehead. By following the feminist logic, she opens herself up to exploitation that "no 'patriarch' of the traditional family would ever impose upon his wife." In giving herself away for nothing in exchange, a woman's "classical power to challenge the young man to 'man up' is consumed and lost."[28]

The Power of Pink

As we saw previously, it's no secret that women are slaves to fashion and the dictates of other women. This is nothing new. For one thousand years, Chinese girls were subjected to the agonizing process of foot-binding. The rite of passage first started when a girl was five or six: any younger and it was too painful, any older and the foot was too long. The practice was first a sign of allurement for the opposite sex and later took on a sort of national pride when outsiders tried to ban the grisly practice.

In a similar but even more horrifying way, abortion takes what had been a healthy heart and distorts it into something almost unrecognizable, as when Wendy Davis—to abundant national acclaim—sported her pink sneakers to filibuster a bill that would block late term abortions. When nearly the entire media class and a large portion of the population think it is permissible to kill a viable baby for any reason whatsoever, what is fashionable has definitely trumped what is rational.

The one essential to all the cultural fads, however, is the free and easy access to abortion, since women cannot be man-like if they have to be women; that is, mothers. And so the women of Planned Parenthood thrive off of the myth

---

28   Quoted by Margaret Harper McCarthy, *Torn Asunder* (Grand Rapids, MI: William B. Eerdmans Publishing, 2017), 244.

that women must be like men and that our children are often the enemy who stifle and undermine our pursuit of happiness. They carefully craft a message of compassion, empowerment, and "the sky will fall if we don't have this" rhetoric, slowly leading us to believe in the power of their kind of pink.

So much so that the independent woman who finds herself pregnant will think, "This baby cannot be, for it isn't who I am." The young women without means or with pressure from others will think, "This baby cannot be, for it isn't who I am allowed to be." And the mother of the less than perfect baby (or the baby who isn't the right sex) will think, "This baby cannot be, for he isn't who I want him to be." That's the power of pink.

Like abortion, foot-binding was foisted upon women by other women. "The truth, no matter how unpalatable, is that foot-binding was experienced, perpetuated and administered by women." It did, however, finally come to an end. "Though utterly rejected in China now, . . . it survived for a thousand years in part because of women's emotional investment in the practice."[29]

One day something similar will be said about abortion: it was finally defeated when women realized that they didn't need to maintain the emotional (or financial) investment in the practice. Until then, the cultural chaos that has been sown because of the rejection of motherhood will continue

---

[29]   Amanda Foreman, "Why Footbinding Persisted in China for a Millennium," *Smithsonian*, February 2015, https://www.smithsonianmag.com/history/why-footbinding-persisted-china-millennium-180953971/.

to leave everyone confused about how to live and who to be. As every woman knows, fashion always has a price.

Part III

Mary, the Antidote

CHAPTER 7

The True Mother

"Virgin Mother, daughter of your Son,
humbler and loftier past creation's measure,
the fulcrum of the everlasting plan,
You are she who ennobled human nature
so highly, that its Maker did not scorn
to make Himself the creature of His creature."

—Dante Alighieri

In 1963, Betty Friedan wrote *The Feminine Mystique*. In it, she attempts to describe the issue that is plaguing women of the West and their dissatisfaction with being wives and mothers. She wrote:

> If I am right, the problem that has no name stirring in the minds of so many American women today is not a matter of loss of femininity or too much education, or the demands of domesticity. It is far more important than anyone recognizes. It is the key to these other new and old problems which have been torturing women

and their husbands and children, and puzzling their doctors and educators for years. It may well be the key to our future as a nation and a culture. We can no longer ignore that voice within women that says: "I want something more than my husband and my children and my home."[1]

What Friedan described is an interesting snapshot about women of her time, but there is something about it that she missed. What she described as "the ache with no name" actually has a name. What she unwittingly describes rests deep in our souls—an ache for God. "The feminist movement had its spiritual roots in the dullness and the narrowness of the middle-class family," said Gertrud von le Fort. "From the need of the unfulfilled souls the women of that period cried out for spirit and for love."[2] Friedan and the many women who followed her mistook the object of this universal hunger in the human soul to be something other than God. Missing this key piece of data could only happen by people living in a theologically illiterate culture, who simply don't know, or misinterpreted, the stories told by our predecessors that helped us identify this nameless-ache. The Jewish Friedan probably didn't know St. Augustine's "Our hearts are made for you, O Lord, and they are restless until they rest in you." But she also seems to not have known quotes that respond to this ache in her own faith tradition:

---

[1]   Betty Friedan, *The Feminine Mystique* (W.W. Norton and Company, 2013), Kindle Edition, chapter 1.

[2]   Gertrud von le Fort, *The Eternal Woman* (San Francisco: Ignatius Press, 2010), 56.

"For he satisfies him who is thirsty, and the hungry he fills with good things" (Ps 107:9), or "For I will satisfy the weary soul, and every languishing soul I will replenish" (Jer 31:25). Friedan did not discover something new, what was new was that she just didn't know what she discovered.

What is the antidote, then, to this ache without a name? God, of course, but particularly for women, the unique relationship *every* woman has to be his beloved daughter. This is why Mary offers us the best model of what it means to be a woman, because she surrendered every piece of herself to God the Father as a beloved daughter.

Mary knew the truth about herself: that everything she had, everything she was, and everything she would ever do was because of the gifts offered to her by her Father, her Creator. She not only knew the truth about herself—which has made her the humblest woman to ever live—but she also knew the truth about God, who he is, especially as Father and Creator.

The human heart aches for God, but the female heart aches for some very specific things: to know the truth of who we are and secure a recognition of our dignity, a longing to be fruitful or to do what is good, and a desire to be beautiful. These desires run deep in a woman's soul. They don't just stem from a superficial place, but are gifted to us by God. The only way that they can truly be satisfied is to surrender them back to God. One of the concepts that will be considered in this chapter, as well as chapters 8 and 9, is the recognition that we are created in God's image and likeness so that when we live lives that are surrendered to him, his attributes can shine through us. It is sin that deforms us, but sanctity restores our wholeness to living truth, goodness, and beauty without tarnish. When our will is put aside and we take up the will of God, then he will be seen in us, in our being, actions, and beauty. This is the reality of Mary: that she is the truest reflection of God who ever lived—other than her Son—so her existence reveals great truths about God. Mary's purity allows the essence of God to shine through her. The title for the nameless ache posed by Friedan and other women becomes remarkably clear when we start to understand exactly who Mary is.

The Most Powerful Woman in the World

For many, Mary remains a silent, still statue, locked in a saccharine pose, tucked away in a side altar of a church. There is much more to this woman, however, that goes well beyond our contemporary impression of her.

In 2015, National Geographic called her the most powerful woman in the world. Journalist Maureen Orth explained:

> Mary is everywhere: Marigolds are named for her. Hail Mary passes save football games. The image in Mexico of Our Lady of Guadalupe is one of the most reproduced female likenesses ever. Mary draws millions each year to shrines such as Fatima, in Portugal, and Knock, in Ireland, sustaining religious tourism estimated to be worth billions of dollars a year and providing thousands of jobs. She inspired the creation of many great works of art and architecture (Michelangelo's "Pietà," Notre Dame Cathedral), as well as poetry, liturgy, and music (Monteverdi's *Vespers for the Blessed Virgin*). And

she is the spiritual confidante of billions of people, no matter how isolated or forgotten.[3]

She has been hailed as the most powerful woman in the world; the most painted, photographed, and prayed to throughout human history. For centuries, children were named for her, songs were sung for her, gardens were grown for her, battles fought for her, sacrifices made for her.

Joseph Cardinal Mindszenty (1892–1975), who was imprisoned first by the Nazis and then by the Communists in Hungary for twenty-three years, said of her, "Veneration of Mary is the great genius which gives Christianity its power, courage, and victoriousness."[4]

Not just another saint, she is *the* saint. It was only through her *fiat*, her yes in willingly accepting the motherhood of God, that Jesus was able to come into the world. Anglican convert Blessed John Henry Cardinal Newman described Mary as our "happier world." By leading her children to her Son, the Blessed Mother helps "them to regain that which has been lost through the fall and sin. She rids us of false teaching. Far from a saccharine devotion, Mary burns through the vices of the cynic, the jaded, the angry, the agitated and the hopeless. In their place, she plants the gifts of peace, order, hope, strength, goodness, and creativity."[5]

---

[3]   Maureen Orth, "How the Virgin Mary Became the World's Most Powerful Woman," *National Geographic*, December 8, 2015, http://ngm.nationalgeographic.com/2015/12/virgin-mary-text.

[4]   Josef Cardinal Mindszenty, *The Face of the Heavenly Mother* (New York: Philosophical Library, 1951), 85.

[5]   Carrie Gress, *The Marian Option* (Charlotte: TAN Books, 2016), 27.

The Blessed Mother is a kind of safeguard to help Christians remain close to Christ. Many of the devout and faithful have discarded her, believing that devotion to her is an offense to Christ, but millennia of faithful offer a different view. "Son and Mother went together," said Cardinal Newman, "and the experience of three centuries has confirmed their testimony, for Catholics who have honoured the Mother, still worship the Son, while Protestants, who now have ceased to confess the Son, began then by scoffing at the Mother."[6] Far from an obstacle to her Son, she is the portal through whom so many faithful have been brought closer to him. Saint Bridget of Sweden was told by the Blessed Virgin, "My son and I redeemed the world as with one heart." To embrace her Immaculate Heart is to simultaneously embrace his Sacred Heart.

For centuries, she has been a lightning rod of the Christian faith, more controversial than even her Son. During the English Reformation in the sixteenth century, painting after painting of the Madonna were tossed on bonfires to get rid of any of the "popish" scent still wafting over the English Channel. During the eighteenth-century French Revolution, there were many vile desecrations of Our Lady, including the renaming of Notre Dame Cathedral as the Temple of Reason, dedicated to the Goddess of Liberty, while her statues were destroyed, and prostitutes were put on display on the altars. Then in the twentieth century, in Soviet Russia, the Church of Our Lady of Kazan, in Red Square in then

---

6   John Henry Cardinal Newman, "The Glories of Mary for the Sake of Her Son," *The Newman Reader:* http://www.newmanreader. org/works/discourses/discourse17.html.

Leningrad (St. Petersburg), was destroyed and replaced with a tribute to Soviet communism. These famous revolutions did not, however, have the last word when it came to Our Lady. Time and again, she has triumphed over her enemies.

Mary's relationship with her rival goddesses has been no different than these relatively modern enemies, starting with the patron goddess of Mary's adopted town, Ephesus, following Christ's crucifixion. Some traditions tell us that she and St. John moved there, where they lived out the rest of their lives in a humble home halfway between the sea and a mountain top. Her home, rediscovered in the 1800s and carefully excavated during times of peace, can still be visited today.

The virgin goddess Artemis (known to the Romans as Diana), currently being resurrected by the goddess movement, was the most powerful goddess in the Roman world. Her temple at Ephesus is known as one of the seven wonders of the ancient world. When St. Paul preached in Ephesus, he was driven out of the temple by devotees of Artemis who were worried that Christianity might be bad for their souvenir sales. It seemed that, for a time, the virgin goddess had the upper hand over Christianity, but eventually the temple was destroyed in AD 401. Then just thirty years later, Our Lady was proclaimed the Mother of God in the same city at the Council of Ephesus. Cyril of Alexandria, who convened the council in place of the pope, joyfully announced to the locals chanting in the streets, "Mother of God! Mother of God!" that after much debate, Mary had indeed been proclaimed the Mother of God. He described Mary to them as "the Mother of God, the holy ornament of all the universe, the unquenchable lamp, the crown of virginity, the scepter, the container of the uncontainable, mother and virgin."[7] It is now Our Lady who is forever associated with Ephesus, as well as St. Paul and his letters to the Ephesians, which are full of tenderness, wisdom, and charity; no doubt a corrective to the lack of faith and vices he witnessed in the ancient city.

Artemis is the not the only goddess Mary has silenced. In Rome, she is honored in the church of *Santa Maria Sopra Minerva*, or Our Lady Over Minerva (known as the goddess Athena in Greek). The church to Our Lady was built over the ruins of a temple honoring Minerva. Our Lady of Victory, or Victory-Bearer, had been a title of Athena. It was given to Our Lady after many successful battles where an icon of her was venerated or the Rosary was prayed for Christians to be victorious, such as the battle of Lepanto or one of the sieges of Constantinople. And a stone's throw from this church is the Pantheon, formerly a temple to all gods but now dedicated to St. Mary and all the martyrs.

Even Our Lady's apparitions on Tepeyac Hill to St. Juan Diego involved conquering one or, possibly, two different goddesses worshipped by the blood-thirsty Aztecs: the relatively benign goddess Quezalcoatl and the more vicious Cōātlīcue, known as the "devouring mother," who wore a "skirt of snakes" and a necklace made of human hearts, hands, and skulls. Mary's apparition, which converted an estimated four to ten million natives, put an end to any type of goddess worship of that era. (Life Tip: Avoid the woman

---

7   Warren H. Carroll, *The Building of Christendom*, vol. 2 (Front Royal: Christendom College Press, 1987), 94.

or goddess who is holding or wearing a snake. Things never go well when there is a snake.)

As I explained in my book *The Marian Option,* while many consider Our Lady to be weak and saccharine, she is no wilting daisy. A ninth-century priest wrote that Mary "is called terrible as an army arrayed for battle."[8] Many of Mary's titles speak to her capacity to defend the Church and Christians; history has witnessed her "terrible" saving power over and over again throughout the centuries.

But even given her status as a warrior against her enemies, Our Lady is a warm and tender mother to us all. At the foot of the cross, through the horrible laboring of Calvary, she accepted us as her children: "'Woman, behold your son!' Then he said to the disciple, 'Behold, your mother!' And from that hour the disciple took her to his own home" (Jn 19:25–27). As a demon commanded to tell the truth tells us, "In an instant, she loved all her children for all generations and said her second 'yes.' After her 'yes' to the Angel, she said her 'yes' to her son on the Cross so that you would all become her children."[9] She loves us with the perfect love of a perfect mother, responding to all the needs of her children with compassion and care.

The Woman and the Goddesses

Our Lady is not a goddess, but a woman. Who she is, however, is far beyond the wildest imagining of our pagan and even Jewish ancestors. Up until the point of Mary of

---

8   Quoted in Bamonte, *Virgin Mary and Exorcism,* 66.
9   Bamonte, *Virgin Mary and Exorcism,* 122.

Nazareth's entry into history, every goddess had some sort of Achilles' heel plaguing her, a vice that would confound her. Never had there been a perfect woman. It was a radically new thing that entered into fallen human history when God gave us a woman—a mortal woman, not a goddess—who was both sinless and perfect, without a major vice weighing her down. It is an idea that could only have been given to us by God. Yes, there were goddesses who had the title of Queen of Heaven, or who were stars over the sea, or virgins, or mothers of divinity, but never was there a woman who was both a virgin *and* a mother, and *not* a goddess. In Our Lady, God gave us something truly unique. Ironically, it is the woman, not the goddess, who is perfect and immortal, mother to all, and Mother of God.

As a result of this unique call, the Mother of God has the titles of many ancient goddesses because she was who others had hoped the goddesses would be. They were archetypes of the kind of perfection dreamed of but never made a reality until Mary of Nazareth arrived in the world. Our Lady triumphed over these clay-footed goddesses and was given their misplaced titles because she truly was the only one worthy of them; titles such as Queen of Heaven, Star of the Sea, Seat of Wisdom, the Mother of God, and Madonna, among others. She is not only a well-behaved woman who made history but the best-behaved woman around whom all of history turns.

Mary Power

One of the reasons Our Lady is wildly neglected is because her type of empowerment isn't clothed in the typical garb: she isn't outspoken, assertive, or intimidating; she isn't protesting topless in the streets; and she isn't donning a pink hat to show her power and conformity to feminist fads. Her approach is much different, and it can be a hard sell in the current climate. Our Lady's virtues are the exact opposite of what the world has been promoting for decades. Few are willing to tell women to be obedient, humble, submissive, and meek, which is probably why we don't hear it very often. None of these fit very neatly into a sound bite, and even if they did, most women don't have the moral experience to know how they look in practical life. These virtues smack of a "doormat woman." And yet these virtues, like Mary's Son, are "the stone the builders rejected"; they are the virtues we ignore at our own peril. Yes, it all sounds a little crazy to our modern ears and sensibilities, but because of who Mary is, they are most worthy of consideration. Mary's "vocation is to wait, to suggest and respond, *to be*, far more than *to do*," says Dominican theologian Fr. Gerald Vann. Reviewing Mary's life, Fr. Vann described Mary's vocation in more detail:

> So to Mary in her stillness comes the announcement which is to summons to both suffering and glory, and her reply is "So be it"; and her vocation henceforth is to live and work and suffer for the fulfilment of *his* vocation; and she does not command or urge, she suggests: "they have no wine"; when the time comes for him to "go out into the world" she retires into the

background, she waits; and when at the end he needs
her comfort and her strength she gives it, not by saying
anything or doing anything, but by standing silent at
the foot of the cross, by *being* with him.[10]

Ironically, the most powerful woman in the world did very little that people would consider important. Her secret was to unite herself to God in order that she might become more while doing less.

Mary's power, then, is in her perfect surrender to God. "Behold, I am the handmaid of the Lord; let it be to me according to your word" (Lk 1:38). Gertrud von le Fort, who wrote deeply about what it means to be a woman, said, "Surrender to God is the only absolute power with which the creature is endowed."[11] The world tells us that we are powerful when we are strong, full of vigor and life, and able to conquer or overcome those who are weaker than we are. Mary's strength is the inverse: "For when I am weak, then I am strong" (2 Cor 12:10). Her strength is in her capacity to get her will out of the way and allow the will of her beloved Father to shine through her. The real power to bring order, love, and a true icon of God is found in the surrender.

Mary's capacity to surrender wasn't because she started off in a place of weakness, von Le Fort explained. Women are not intrinsically weak. Their power, when misused, can wreak havoc on an entire society. If we look at Eve, "the Bible story shows clearly that she was the stronger and had the ascendancy over man." Man is physically stronger,

---

10   Gerald Vann, *The Water and the Fire* (Sheed & Ward, 1954), 137.

11   von le Fort, *Eternal Woman*, xv.

but women have a different kind of strength. "Whenever woman has been suppressed," von Le Fort continues, "it was never because she was weak, but because she was recognized and feared as having power, and with reason; for at the moment when the stronger power no longer desires surrender but seeks self-glorification, a catastrophe is bound to ensue."[12] When a woman rejects the authority of men, of her husband, that God has placed above her—as we have seen, to protect women from the abuse of their own power—her refusal carries with it something of the demonic, von Le Fort says, because it brings the "seduction of the self-will."[13] A woman under the spell of her own will is unable to see clearly the will of the Father, or of her husband, or her children, resulting in the upheaval we see in our own culture, and it is particularly children who are on the chopping block in sacrifice to the will of the mother.

Surrender in the right sense can only happen when a woman knows the person she is surrendering to is trustworthy, loves her unconditionally, and always does what is best for her. This is why parents are so vitally important to the faith of children if they are to grow into healthy adults. If children do not get these gifts from parents, then their capacity to understand how much the Father loves them will be deeply damaged. Parents are the bridge between a child and God; they are the first icon of his unconditional love. Without good parents, faith in an all-loving, benevolent father is very challenging. And *vice versa*, as Cardinal

---

[12] Ibid., 13.
[13] Ibid., 14.

Mindszenty pointed out, "For when men no longer understand the infinite charity of God, they will no longer prize
the most striking revelation of that charity, the love of mothers."[14] This helps explain why the women behind the feminist movement, who had troubled relationships with their
mothers, also had little faith. And when we lose faith in an
all loving and benevolent God, we feel the need to make
ourselves gods, to protect ourselves from vulnerabilities at
the hands of others who might wound us, even those who
claim to love us. Self-willing, controlling others, and the
myriad of other ways women reject surrendering to God's
will are deeply rooted in the damaged faith that misunder-
stands how wide and deep God's love is for each one of us.
Mary's surrender is based upon the reality that she knows she
is loved, and she has no shame, no fear, no emptiness in her
soul, no wounds of rejection or abandonment that compel
her to keep something for herself the way that the rest of
humanity does.

Of course, those who had bad parents are not left
orphans. God can overcome any wound of the heart. Mary,
our mother in the order of grace, along with the Father, will
never leave us orphans. As one theologian wrote, "Mary
helps Christians understand with what tenderness they are
embraced by God."[15] And so among Mary's titles is Mother
of Orphans.

---

[14]   Mindszenty, *The Face of the Heavenly Mother,* 103.
[15]   *André* Feuillet, *Jesus and His Mother* (Petersham, MA: St. Bede's
        Publication, 1984), 209.

She Fights Like a Mom

Mary's power is truly that of a mother, but a perfect mother whose will is directly aligned with God's perfect will. Our Lady, Pope John Paul II wrote, "participates maternally in the tough fight against the powers of darkness that unfold during the whole of human history."[16] How would a mother do this? Through fierce protection of her children, but also through order, discipline, education, love, assistance, and particularly by being present to them and suffering with them.

There is a unique testimony to Mary's witness at Calvary to which every maternal heart can relate. It came from an unusual source: a demon commanded to tell the truth about Mary by a priest during an exorcism (which is why some of the grammar is odd). Speaking of what he saw at Calvary, the demon said:

> That One was always there with tears that flowed without stopping and with eyes turned toward the face of her son to collect every little, every little, every little suffering. She lived his passion in her heart. The sword was piercing her Heaaaart! The blood of the Son and the heart of the Mamma flowed. She was always there, tormented by pain but most beautiful in her suffering. Ahhh! She shone with pain and prayer: 'May your will be done. May your will be done.' Never did she lower her face. Only when He died [did she lower it] when the whole world moved. She [in that moment] was

---

[16]   John Paul II, *Redemptoris Mater*, no. 47.

firm. She did not move. She knew what was happening. She knew that it would happen that God would feel her pain for her son. Her eyes were fixed on those of the Son, fixed. And she looked at him, looked at all his wounds, looked at the blood that was flowing from his head. And she wanted to clean his face, caress his hair, kiss his wounds, that broken nose, that swollen face. And she said, 'What have they done to you, my dear!? You who love everyone! May your will be done, Father! Your will, Father! Father, the nails! Those most beautiful hands have prayed, have healed, have blessed. Father, those holy hands! Poor hands! And the arms . . . See Father, what pain! He who is your son, Sooooon . . . Father, may your will be done! Those feet that have walked so much, those feet that have walked so much, walked so much, how they were beautiful when they were so little! How many times I kissed them! How many times I kissed them! Make me kiss them also as they are! Full of blood, Father! Tell him that I am here! Tell him that I love him! That I understand him! That I am with him, that I suffer with him![17]

What mother can't relate to kissing her son's beautiful feet when he was little? What mother doesn't want her son to know that she is with him through every suffering?

And yet, Mary is not just another mother. The demons tell us much more: "There is no tongue to praise the Mother of God as she merits. There is no creature who can understand

---

[17]   Bamonte, *Virgin Mary and Exorcism*, 122.

her greatness, her goodness, her power. Mary has more power herself than all the angels, all the creatures, all the saints together. There is nothing comparable to Mary."[18]

Such a testimony lines up with what others have said about her. Hildegard von Bingen, the eleventh-century nun, polymath, and a doctor of the Church, wrote of Mary, "She is so bright and glorious that you cannot look at her face or her garments for the splendor with which she shines. For she is terrible with the terror of the avenging lightning, and gentle with the goodness of the bright sun; and both her terror and her gentleness are incomprehensible to humans. . . . But she is with everyone and in everyone, and so beautiful is her secret that no person can know the sweetness with which she sustains people, and spares them in inscrutable mercy.[19]

Despite her splendor, Our Lady does not make herself a celebrity, she does not draw attention to herself, but is always saying, "Do whatever he tells you" (Jn 2:5). She isn't seeking to be worshipped, but only to bring her spiritual children to her Son.

The saddest reality about the women's movement, particularly many of the founders of it, is that Our Lady is the true mother they needed. Instead, they chose terrible counterfeits that could never bring the love, affection, healing—the mothering—for which their hearts longed.

---

[18]   Ibid., 42.

[19]   Hildegard of Bingen's vision of the Feminine Divine, from *Scivias*, III, 4.15, translated by Mother Columba Hart, O.S.B. and Jane Bishop.

CHAPTER 8

Fruit and Content

"The tree that is beside the running water
is fresher and gives more fruit."

—St. Teresa of Avila

Three women were recently featured in a secular magazine. They were, by most standards, normal, well-adjusted secular women—they had exciting and adventurous jobs, plenty of money in the bank, and men at their disposal. They seemed to be living the feminist dream. And yet, they all said there was something missing. One said she felt the urge to just bake bread, another wanted to grow a garden, a third said she felt like quitting her job and raising a bunch of children. There was something deeper that these women wanted to grow, make, nurture, and love. No one had told them, however, that this wasn't the way the feminist playbook was supposed to go—their human nature, their "existential slip," was showing right there among the glossy pages.

A recurrent thread in this book is the contempt directed at virginity and motherhood by the anti-Marian spirit of our age. After fifty years of watching the sterility of feminism destroy the culture, there is plenty of evidence that purity, virginity, and motherhood are important not just to women but to families and societies. It is precisely these things that the women's movement has trampled upon in the name of progress and liberation. Women's strength or power, our surrender, doesn't mean being inactive or idle. It is another one of the deep mysteries of God that women are simultaneously receptive *and* actively bringing about the good in the lives of others. Women were made to be fruitful.

As we saw in chapter 5, fertility is something from which women simply cannot run away; those who try end up abusing it instead of honoring it. But what does it look like to actually honor our fertility? What does it look like to understand that at the core of every woman's heart—though it may be buried under abuse, contempt, ignorance, or misunderstanding—is the desire to be fruitful, to be a vessel, spiritually and physically, for others to find strength, care, affirmation, charity, nurturing, and home. Fertility is the desire to do good things. Edith Stein said that women "fulfill themselves by giving something of their own life so that others may live."[1]

Nobel laureate William Golding, author of *The Lord of the Flies*, has a tight but colorful description of just what women are able to do when they understand their own fertility, their

---

[1]   Edith Stein, *Woman: Collected Works*, vol. 2, trans. Freda Mary Oben (Washington, DC: ICS Publications, 1996), 51.

own fruitfulness, and how it creates or improves the lives of others. He says, "I think women are foolish to pretend they are equal to men, they are far superior and always have been. Whatever you give a woman, she will make greater. If you give her sperm, she'll give you a baby. If you give her a house, she'll give you a home. If you give her groceries, she'll give you a meal. If you give her a smile, she'll give you her heart. She multiplies and enlarges what is given to her."[2]

Golding's insight is rich and beautiful. As we saw earlier, women are called to "contain" others, not just to hold onto them, but to improve them and let them go again, now healthier, stronger, and better prepared for the journey. The time-honored symbols of women—vessels, ovens, ships, and so on—represent containing something, transforming it, bringing people to safety. These are not unimportant things, but truly the elements that help people grow into their full potential.

The Lesson of the Farmer

More than two thousand years ago, Roman senator and famed orator Cicero first coined the term *cultura anima*, or "cultivating the soul." What he meant by it was "to foster what nature grants"; that is, to acknowledge that by nature there is a certain way things will grow best and certain ways to guarantee that something won't grow at all.

---

[2]   "Golding's Introduction to Lord of the Flies," AbecedariusRex, video, 2:40, May 22, 2010, https://www.youtube.com/watch?-time_continue=21&v=vYnfSV27vLY.

Joel Salatin is a man that knows a lot about farming. Called the world's most innovative farmer by *Time* magazine, Salatin has been featured in books and films like *The Omnivore's Dilemma* and *Food, Inc.* for his practices that are changing the way people think about food. While his approach may seem radical (no antibiotics, no growth hormones), his farming practices are fundamentally about working with nature instead of against it. And it all starts with soil. Salatin, like most farmers, knows that soil health is crucial. "Stimulating soil biota is our first priority," says Salatin. "Soil health creates healthy food."[3] Farmers like him are relearning how "to foster what nature grants."

A priest raised on a farm wanted to help promote vocations to the priesthood. He knew, like Salatin, how to grow things, and the first place to start was with the soil. If seeds didn't have good soil, nothing could grow properly. When it came to vocations, then, what exactly was the soil?

Mothers.

So he got to work, beginning with the soil. He first started a women's Bible study. Then he started a couple's Bible study. Then he moved on to the men, then fathers and sons, mothers and daughters, and finally, he started a group for the young people. The farmer priest knew that vocations were the fruit of good families, but particularly of good mothers supported by strong husbands. All of these pieces are integral.

---

3   Joel Salatin, "Principles of Polyface Farm," http://www.polyface-farms.com/principles/.

What, then, does the enemy do? He steals the heart of the woman, steals the goodness from the soil and poisons it. He whispers, "Contraception will make you free. You don't need to have children. Children are a luxury you cannot afford." He continues, "Children just get in the way of happiness. Let someone else take care of them." And on and on. And women have listened. We have been listening intently and telling others, while ignoring the misery that plagues us. The farmer priest's wisdom isn't unique to him. Archbishop Fulton Sheen wrote, "When a man loves a woman, it follows that the nobler the woman, the nobler the love; the higher the demands made by the woman, the more worthy a man must be. That is why woman is the measure of the level of our civilization."[4] Truly, the level to which women aspire is the level that men will reach for, but if women don't aspire to anything, the men won't either. As Mae West said, "Whenever women go wrong, men go right after them."

This general idea is not unique to Western civilization; even Confucius is known to have said, "Where the woman is faithful, no evil can befall. The woman is the root and the man is the tree. The tree grows only as high as the root is strong."[5]

This understanding of soil underscores the tight link connecting a woman's respect for her physical fertility—both in virginity and maternity—to the health of her soul and fruitfulness of her actions.

---

[4]   Fulton J. Sheen, *The World's First Love*, 2nd ed. (San Francisco: Ignatius Press, 2010), 184.

[5]   Alice von Hildebrand, *The Privilege of Being a Woman* (Ave Maria, Florida: Sapientia Press, 2002), 28.

Understanding women's desire for fruitfulness sheds a new light on Adam and Eve. As we saw above, Adam, like most men, didn't want to fight his wife. Betraying God, he took the fruit Eve offered instead of battling her. But we also see that Eve is every woman—she is reaching for fruit. She is trying to be fruitful. Like Eve, every woman has the option to reach for the appropriate fruit or the forbidden fruit. However she chooses, because so much depends on her, the consequences are far reaching.

Marian Fertility

Mary has long been considered the virgin soil, dating back even as far as roughly AD 180 when St. Irenaeus of Lyons wrote, "If Adam was created with the help of a virgin soil, not yet tilled, by the virtue and power of God (Gn 2:4–7), the new Adam also must draw his origin from a virgin soil, by the same power and virtue of God. Mary is this virgin soil from whom Christ became the 'first-born.'"[6]

Mary's maternity is not accidental; she wasn't just a body that carried the Son of God, but much more than that. Her openness to the will of God, her yes, was what allowed her to be the perfect model of femininity. In a similar way that Mary expressed the truth about God and herself—his greatness and her humility—through her perfection, her fertility expresses the goodness of God. God is all good, and only through the perfect woman can his goodness be seen perfectly. Our Lady's goodness can only exist because of the goodness of God. This is how she "magnifies" the Lord—she

---

[6]   Irenaeus of Lyons, *Against Heresies*, III 18,7 I.

makes visible the invisible goodness of God—as she says in the Magnificat prayer.

She was everything—and the only woman who has ever been all of these things—virgin and mother, pure, immaculate. Because she was incorrupt, perfect, and pure, there was no dis-integration in her. Her soul and body were united so the fruitfulness that was happening in her body was simultaneously happening in her soul. Body and soul, then, worked together to express the fruitfulness that comes with being the Mother of God.

By honoring her own virginity, a woman imitates Mary. And by honoring her own maternity, a woman also imitates Mary. In imitating her, women can share in her remarkable fruitfulness, both in their own souls and bodies, their families, and society. No wonder, then, that Satan would attack a woman's purity, that he would try to poison the ground that God hallowed, the very means through which women can truly be fruitful, both physically and spiritually.

Faux Fruit From Bad Soil

Before looking at the patterns of good fruit in the lives of women, we can see the desire for fruitfulness even among those furthest from God. Phyllis Chesler, as we saw earlier, described the activities of the early feminists, "We picketed, marched, protested, sat in, and famously took over offices and buildings; helped women obtain illegal abortions; . . . condemned incest, rape, sexual harassment, and domestic violence; organized speak-outs, crisis hotlines, and shelters for battered women"[7] Within this list, edited slightly from the original, there are a lot of ways in which these women were actively trying to help other women. This is what motivated them, by large measure. What's striking here is that—even when their intentions are separated from what is objectively good, which is the case with every anti-Marian movement—the underlying desire to be helpful, to give to others, to make a difference, to be fruitful, remains. This is what motivates social justice warriors and virtue signalers: they want to do good and to have others do good. They are just confused about what good *is*. Clearly, they are is misguided: in most cases, the assistance they offer is like adding a match to a gas leak. But the fundamental desires of the female heart are consistent.

Taking this point a step further, it is also fair to say that women generally have a fundamental desire to nurture. Sadly, we can also be remarkably misguided in what we choose to nurture. Instead of nurturing children or spiritual children, our nurturing can embrace something intangible, such as a grudge, anger, victimization, resentment, or pain. "We can hold our traumas tightly, perpetually nursing them," Noelle Mering wrote, "and in so doing elevate ourselves to a special status where only we, who've suffered mightily, might enter. Our trauma can become both trophy and weapon."[8] For the more narcissistic woman, she might nurture her career,

---

[7]   Chesler, *Politically Incorrect*, 87.

[8]   Noelle Mering, "Here's the Danger of Weaponizing Legitimate Suffering for Revenge," *The Federalist*, October 10, 2018, https://thefederalist.com/2018/10/10/heres-danger-weaponizing-legitimate-suffering-revenge/.

her figure, her bank account, her adventures, or her sexual exploits. This deep desire is also what is driving the pet craze in our culture, one that has led Americans to spend half a billion dollars on pet costumes for Halloween, to name just one of the outrageous animal expenditures,[9] while folks in Virginia made sure shelter animals had a place to go to for Thanksgiving.[10] Women must nurture *something*.

Real Fruit From Rich Soil

Women desire fruitfulness in our lives, and we desire to bring life, light, goodness, health, and salvation into the lives of those we love. What we scarcely understand on an intellectual level is that there is a deep relationship between a woman's fruitfulness—what she does that improves the lives of others around her—and how she treats her own fertility and purity. We are embodied souls, not merely "meat" envelopes laboring through life from one pleasure or desire to the next. Our souls animate our bodies, as the two are intimately connected. How we treat one affects the way we treat the other. When we respect the body, the soul is better ordered; when we build up the soul, the body is likewise ennobled. By targeting a woman's physical fertility, the anti-Marian

---

9 Andrew Keshner, "Pet Owners will Spend Half a Billion Dollars on Animal Costumes This Halloween," *Market Watch*, October 16, 2018, https://www.marketwatch.com/story/instagram-loving-pets-owners-will-spend-nearly-500m-on-animal-costumes-this-halloween-2018-10-16.

10 Meghan Overdeep, "Virginia Families Are Hosting Shelter Dogs for Thanksgiving," *Southern Living*, November 16, 2018, https://www.southernliving.com/news/richmond-animal-shelter-thanksgiving-fosters.

spirit is able to deform the entire woman. When virginity and maternity are tossed aside as petty and inconsequential, the woman slowly disintegrates; her efforts become sterile, her relationships empty, and her soul searches under every rock, shopping mall, or fad for something to fill it up again.

Because fertility is a defining character of a woman, it should not be too surprising to discover that our physical fruitfulness is an outward reflection of our inward fruitfulness. If we look at holy women who are "interiorly fruitful," we will discover that, despite all the superficial differences, a strikingly common pattern emerges. A woman goes to prayer, and during that time of silence and being present to the Lord, a tiny idea is planted in her heart. It is so small and seems so insignificant that she may even dismiss it. She tells no one about it, and yet whatever it is, this idea delights her, sets her heart on fire, draws her deeper into prayer.

Eventually, that little idea grows as the woman nurtures it, year after year. Eventually, it takes on a life of its own, one that she helps to guide and bring to maturity. As time passes, the woman realizes that this tiny idea has grown into something independent of her—it has taken on its own life, it is bigger than she is, and far surpasses anything she could have previously imagined. We can see an example of this in St. Teresa of Calcutta's life. She was in her forties when she decided to leave the convent in Ireland and head to India. Her little idea to help the poorest of the poor led to the Missionaries of Charity, which has a life all its own that has far outlived the little Albanian nun who birthed the order into life.

Curiously, this process of interior fruitfulness looks an awful lot like the process of pregnancy. A tiny seed is planted. Initially, the mother is the only one aware of the new life within her. Time, great care, love, and sacrifice eventually bring a child to life, a child who will eventually have a life of his own, no longer needing the mother for his life to continue. The pattern of physical birth closely resembles the process of spiritual birth to which women are called. This beautiful pattern speaks clearly of the kind of relationship women are called to have with the Trinity—a fruitful one, where the woman is receptive to the seed of an idea and then nurtures it, helps it to grow and become something beyond her imagination—just like the children mothers give life to physically.

So, as we have seen, the physical fruitfulness we see in our bodies is a symbol of the fruitfulness available to us in our souls. But like anything else, this fruitfulness has to happen in accordance with nature, to "foster what nature grants," for there actually to be good fruit, both natural and supernatural.

What happens, then, when women act without God? The first half of this book gave us plenty of examples. When women don't act in accord with grace and nature, an entry point is opened for the devil to come in and wreak havoc on their lives. As Gertrud von Le Fort wrote, "without eternal loyalties, we lose not only eternity, but this life as well."[11] The woman that does not have God at the center of her life will place her heart, her soul, and her efforts at the service of

---

[11]   von Le Fort, *Eternal Woman*, 59.

something else. In previous ages, like when von Le Fort was writing, misguided loyalties were typically directed at men. Our own age has unleashed all sorts of options and activism which women prioritize over God, not realizing the barrenness of their actions.

Women long for meaning in our lives and for a sense of mission, both of which have been placed there by God and point to the hunger we have for him. The culture has left us confused about what is truly fulfilling, so most of us don't know where to start beyond picking up the Bible or heading back to Mass. But what we miss, again because it is unfashionable, is that we simply must open ourselves up to God through active receptivity. The model for our fruitfulness and the spiritual shortcut back to God is imprinted in our bodies. We were made to allow God to plant beautiful things in our souls and then to help them grow. A woman's holiness and fruitfulness are directly related to how she treats her fertility and purity. Yes, certainly, men are called to purity, but women have a deeper need for purity because of their capacity to bear children and its deep connection to her own fruitfulness.

Labor's Lessons

Women, however, must not merely value purity or maternity for prudish or prideful reasons. Certainly, the human heart has a way of distorting even the best of things. To keep these values in the right order, we have to remember the cross. Our souls are fruitful when we allow the crucified Christ to dwell within us. Our fruitfulness is connected with the cross and cannot happen apart from it. The cross, however, is not just misery and pain. Like laboring to deliver a child, suffering is somehow different when it is "pain with a purpose." The unique message of Catholicism is the recognition that our pain is not in vain, that there are reasons for it. We may not always know what they are, but again, when we are confident in the love Our Father has for us, it's easy to trust in his plan and providential care.

Additionally, the saints speak of a great joy even despite— or because of—great suffering. Their suffering becomes the currency of love, where they can truly make their love known to God because it isn't attached to pleasure, but sacrifice. In the Mass for the old rite of marriage, the Church reminded marrying couples that "sacrifice is usually difficult and irksome. Only love can make it easy, and perfect love can make it a joy." Growth in love is connected with sacrifice and getting beyond our own vices, which is why motherhood is a natural route for women to become saints. The nature of raising children is meant to scour our souls of the vices we acquired when we were single, while replacing them with the virtues that come from the challenges of rearing children, including patience, perseverance, self-giving, compassion, and charity. But all of these efforts must be plugged into God's grace. Without them, our efforts are like trying to vacuum without plugging the vacuum in.

There remains dramatic confusion about the role of purity and honoring motherhood, even among Christians. This is part of the reason why Protestants allow contraception; they don't understand the deep mystery of fertility, virginity, and motherhood, or of the Virgin Mother herself, whom they often neglect. Because they don't understand or appreciate the gift that Mary offers to us, they cannot access this rich connection between a woman's fertility and the integrity of her soul. Until they see this connection, they will continue to use contraception, and confusion about a woman's role in society and in the Church will remain.

Living Fruit

Our Lady offers tremendous hope to help us transform our anti-Marian culture, but again, the answer to it won't be among the usual suspects. The evangelical answer is hidden in plain sight, for those with eyes to see: it is in the model of saintly women who brought Christianity to us, starting from the earliest days of the faith. Women like Mary Magdalen, Sts. Lucy, Agnes, Cecilia, Perpetua, and Felicity passed along the faith to husbands, children, neighbors, and those who witnessed their martyrdom. There was also Clotilde, who converted her husband, Clovis, introducing Christianity to the Franks, or Princess Dobrawa, who influenced Prince Mieszko, which sparked a conversion that set Catholicism ablaze in Poland. Women have always been instrumental in spreading the faith. This is the kind of fruit that Christ and his mother are calling us to. That call is not to become radical activists or social justice warriors but to take the words of St. Teresa of Calcutta to heart: If you want to change the world, go home and love your family. That is the place to start. We all know the challenge of changing ourselves, so the belief that we can change perfect strangers is overwhelming, but when we live in relationship to others, gentle and subtle changes can take place that truly change the culture, one family at a time. "It is through the mediation of women," a theologian has noted, "that men are increasingly given anew to society."[12] Without women's good influence, society cannot renew itself.

Mary has been called by the saints the "neck" or the "ladder" linking heaven and earth. Every woman is called to be a bridge between her family and heaven. Women are called to spark the flame of the divine in the souls of the men and children they love. Women are called to reveal the best of God's love and give those around them the means to find that love. Again, Christianity is full of saintly women, such as St. Monica, St. Helen, St. Cecilia, and countless others that led their husbands, sons, and daughters to embrace the faith—even in the face of martyrdom.

Far from wall-flowers or door mats, saintly women reveal the uniqueness that emerges in a soul tightly bound up in the love of the Father. Curiously, there is not a secular woman who can meet in any direct way the gifts, stature, and achievements of female saints such as Sts. Hildegard of Bingen, Catherine of Siena, or Teresa of Avila (incidentally, all virgins). When a woman's self-will is erased enough to allow room for God, to become his instrument, that is when the miraculous happens. Both Sts. Bernadette and Teresa of Calcutta referred to themselves in this way—Bernadette as a broom and Teresa as a pencil. Through their erasing of self, of pride, of ego, women saints have achieved much more than even the most lauded of secular women. We look back

---

[12]   Feuillet, *Jesus and His Mother*, 206–7.

and are astonished that women could accomplish so much because women "had no power" in these eras, but only because we are mistaken about the real power that women have—it doesn't come *from* them, but *through* them.

CHAPTER 9

Understanding Mary's Beauty

*"The splendor of a soul in grace is so seductive that
it surpasses the beauty of all created things."*

—St. Thomas Aquinas

It was the opportunity of a lifetime, Leah Darrow thought
to herself, walking up the stairs to the old converted warehouse. As the former contestant on *America's Next Top Model*
prepped for the photo shoot, clothing, scarcely big enough
to warrant hangers, was rolled out for her inspection.
"I'm not really comfortable with these. Do you have something else?" she queried.

"Sure, you can find something else. But you will have to
leave. These are your options," came the dry, biting retort.

Selecting the outfit that appeared to have the most cov-
erage, Leah tried to hide her horror as she put them on and
made her way to the photoshoot, well aware that every eye
was on her mostly naked body.

The camera started clicking, and the photographer, sens-
ing her discomfort, tried to loosen her up. "You look hot!"

he said encouragingly. "All the girls feel like this in the beginning."

Unable to un-frazzle her nerves, Leah made the rookie mistake of looking at the flash as the camera snapped away. Her eyes locked shut as she scrambled to get the world around her back into focus. It was then that it happened. Her eyes still unable to focus, she looked up and saw a vision of Christ. He looked at her with sad eyes, asking what she was offering him. She looked down at her hands. *Nothing.* Her hands were empty. She wasn't giving him anything. "You were made for more," was all she heard, and in her heart, she knew she was done. She finally focused and told the photographer she had to go.

The photographer continued to try to console her, plying her with compliments. "Really, everyone feels like this in the beginning!"

She had a flashback to the day she heard models referred to as "hangers," and then thought to herself, "Objects don't have a problem being used. I never want to get used to being an object."

Leah quickly got dressed and then had to make the longest walk of her life across the expansive warehouse to the exit.

Since cajoling wasn't working, the photographer's anger flared. All the demons were out, and he unloaded. "Who do think you are? We are only doing Tyra Banks a favor, but you are old, ugly, fat. You have cellulite. You are 1,000 percent unf***able! You are only good because we make you good. We have to fix your unf***able looks so you can look f***able!"

His last line expressed the foundation and epitome of the beauty industry at large—it was all about making women objects of sexual desire.

"If you leave here, you will be nothing!" he sneered at her.

"Do you promise?" was her sincere response. She wanted to get as far away from this empty shell of a world as possible.[1]

For women in our culture, beauty weighs heavily upon us as an external criterion that we must strive for. It is, however, an unsatisfiable ideal. The fashion industry, as we saw earlier, sets the standard for what "beautiful" women are supposed to look like. What they mean by beautiful is a whole lot different than what beauty is really meant to be. Here again is the chasm between our culture and Mary, between a "beauty" of sexual objectification and a true beauty that stirs the soul, pulls us out of ourselves, and lifts the heart and mind to the Creator of all things. One is edifying, compelling, and uplifting, the other tawdry, seductive, dehumanizing.

Marian Beauty

While researching my book *The Marian Option*, in every apparition of Mary that I encountered, the visionary said she was the most beautiful woman he or she had ever seen. Initially, I found this detail rather prosaic—of course Our Lady is beautiful—but then the greater importance behind her beauty finally hit me. Mary's beauty is important because it is the outward expression of her complete perfection emanating from God's beauty.

---

[1]   Leah Darrow, phone conversation with the author, August 2018.

It is also easy to underestimate just how beautiful Mary is. The saints help us to comprehend her unfathomable beauty. "She is so beautiful," St. Bernadette reported, "that once you have seen her, you want to die to be able to see her again."[2] St. Therese testified to Our Lady's beauty during her great suffering as a child. Little Therese turned to a statue of Mary near her bed and begged Mary to have pity upon her. "All of a sudden, the statue became alive! The Virgin became beautiful, so beautiful that I could never find words to express it. . . . But what penetrated to the roots of my being was her ravishing smile. At that moment, all my pains vanished."[3] Padre Pio (now St. Pio) was once overheard saying, "Jesus was correct . . . yes, you are beautiful . . . if there were no faith, men would say you are a goddess . . . your eyes are more splendid than the sun . . . mommy. I take pride in you. I love you."[4]

When one visionary asked Mary why she was so beautiful, she responded, "Because I love."

Our Lady brought a new kind of beauty and dignity for women into the world. Up until the fullness of the teaching about her, until Christians understood her as Virgin, Mother, and Queen, the fullness of dignity for women hadn't come into full recognition. She set a new watermark for womanhood. "The man, formerly a tyrant and ruler over the woman," Cardinal Mindszenty explains, "becomes a troubadour and servant of the lady now that the gospel has

---

2   Quoted in Bramonte, *Virgin Mary and Exorcism*, 62.

3   St. Therese of Lisieux, *Story of a Soul, Autobiography* (ICS Publications, 1996), 51.

4   Bamonte, *Virgin Mary and Exorcism*, 62.

come into the world. The spiritual beauty which God's hand has caused to bloom in the dignity of motherhood holds man spellbound. Tyrannous sensuality gives way in woman's presence, because purity, sanctity, and a heavenly radiance encompass her."[5]

Like all of God's gifts, Our Lady's beauty isn't meant just for her. Even if her beauty surpasses all others, she isn't the only woman made to be beautiful. True beauty is not an unattainable ideal, nor is it simply a temptation to vanity. Rather, beauty is what God wills for women. He has placed in women the desire for beauty so that we can reveal his beauty to the world. Women have a unique gift to draw men and children to them—and through them to God—through their beauty.

Women Are Supposed to Be Beautiful

There is a well-known Dostoevsky trope that says, "beauty will save the world." The famous Russian is usually taken to mean beauty found in the material arts. Music, architecture, and sculpture are rightfully being plumbed for their world-saving abilities, particularly how they lead a soul back to God. But there is one stone that has yet to be unturned when considering the role beauty plays in saving the world: women.

The desire to be beautiful is deeply embedded in a woman's soul. How do we know this? Because like we saw with fertility in the last chapter, it is seen in our bodies. Women's bodies are beautiful, no question. They are a timeless theme

---

[5]   Mindszenty, *The Face of the Heavenly Mother*, 89.

in art. But also like the fertile body points to a fertile soul, the beautiful body helps signify the presence of beauty in the soul—when we cultivate it.

Each year, American women spend hundreds of billions of dollars on plastic surgery, cosmetics, and weight loss. While we can scoff at this with Qoheleth and say, "Vanity of vanities!" (Eccl 1:2), perhaps there is something to this that goes deeper than vanity? What if God has put that desire into our hearts for a reason? Even the smallest girl will tell you she wants to be as beautiful as a princess. This isn't just cultural conditioning; it is something universal that sits squarely in the feminine heart.

Women's magazines today offer us a different kind of beauty, a beauty to be used as a superficial means of acquiring other things we want: to allure men, impress our friends, or to be admired. The notion that what is beautiful should point beyond itself to the source of all beauty—the Creator—is far, far away. The hollowed-out beauty that only goes skin-deep makes women like "whitewashed tombs, which outwardly appear beautiful, but within they are full of dead men's bones and all uncleanness" (Mt 23:27). The "beauty" in the fashion industry, as Leah Darrow found out the hard way, is an imitation of beauty, an imitation of love. She describes it as a big stick of cotton candy: looks great, tastes great, but dissolves into nothing. Actually, it dissolves into something worse than nothing because its shallowness roams about infecting others. The woman who seeks beauty without also seeking God ends up "ghostly and banal," von Le Fort says. "A countenance emerges that denotes the complete opposite to the image of God: the faceless mask of womanhood."[6] We see this face daily: sullen, pouty, joyless, serious, without a hint of living character.

The Blind Leading the Blind

As we saw in chapter 6, the matriarchy wields a tremendous amount of influence on everyday women. The bulk of advice women hear on what constitutes happiness or healthy relationships comes from women who are acting from deep brokenness—a brokenness they have passed on to further generations. It is advice that comes from women who have shown themselves to be dishonest, particularly if it serves their political cause, and women who believe firmly that sterile sex trumps any notion of family. Their advice comes from a working environment where manipulation, self-gratification, and narcissism are the norms. Men are play things, gender fluidity is fundamental, and coupling with other women (in the singular or plural) is viewed as exotic or even the ideal. This is the kind of advice that will only redound into further brokenness.

These women and the advice they offer are still operating under the impression that human nature can change. Since women have changed, the argument goes, men must also have changed their desires and interests, or simply have adapted to the new version of women, which look a lot more like them, or are dripping with superficial sensuality. The reality, however, is that men haven't changed that much. Many are just waiting for the boomerang to come back

---

6   von le Fort, *Eternal Woman*, 16.

around and for women to act like women again, but the wait might be long if we keep looking to elite women for advice.

The one place few women consider looking for advice, particularly about relationships, is to men. History offers incredible windows into what men think about women when they aren't afraid to reveal what they really think. Millennia of poetry, music, and literature offer an exquisite picture of what it is in a woman's soul that moves men. From the dawn of time, men have crooned over particular attributes they love about women: loyalty, sweetness, a calming presence, kindness, thoughtfulness. Homer, Dante, Petrarch, the Beatles, Elvis, James Taylor, Sting, the Grateful Dead, Tim McGraw, and on and on—all speak of loving a truthful, kind, loyal, soulful woman who brings them peace. The message from men hasn't changed. Take, for example, this from Shakespeare's "Sonnet 29":

> When, in disgrace with fortune and men's eyes,
> I all alone beweep my outcast state,
> And trouble deaf heaven with my bootless cries,
> And look upon myself and curse my fate,
> Wishing me like to one more rich in hope,
> Featured like him, like him with friends
>   possessed,
> Desiring this man's art and that man's scope
> With what I most enjoy contented least;
> Yet in these thoughts myself almost despising,
> Haply I think on thee, and then my state,
> (Like to the lark at break of day arising
> From sullen earth) sings hymns at heaven's gate;

> For thy sweet love remembered such wealth
>   brings
> That then I scorn to change my state with kings.

Or "She Walks in Beauty" by Lord Byron,

> She walks in Beauty, like the night
> Of Cloudless climes and starry skies;
> And all that's best of dark and bright
> meet in her aspect and her eyes.

These are timeless poems, joining the thousands of songs written for the women who are loved for their goodness, beauty, honesty, and loyalty. Not to mention the women that inspired the likes of poets Dante and Petrarch—Beatrice and Laura—who have served as great muses for the poets of the ages. This sort of "fair" love that exceeds the lowly regions of the soul could not have come about without the role played by the ideal woman: the Virgin Mother and Queen. Contrast this ideal with its opposite. Songs have not been written for nagging, angry, self-absorbed women. These are simply not the qualities that lift men's souls.

Pastor Bill Johnson of the Bethel Church once told a story of how his wife inspires him. "Scripture says I'm supposed to fill my mind with certain things. If I am struggling with that, here is what I do: I will think about my wife because she is everything in verse 8 (Phil 4:4–8)."[7] He continues,

---

[7]   "Finally, brethren, whatever is true, whatever is honorable, whatever is just, whatever is pure, whatever is lovely, whatever is gracious, if there is any excellence, if there is anything worthy of praise, think about these things" (Phil 4:8).

"She . . . is so true, so absolute, so life giving, she is so lovely, and praiseworthy and virtuous. She is so excellent. All those things." Just thinking about her goodness helps him recalibrate, he explains. "I will start to think specifically about [the goodness of my wife] and it is hard to be mad at anybody if I am thinking of those things."[8]

Women's beauty isn't meant to fuel our vanity; it is meant both to reflect the goodness and love of God and also draw those around us to him through our gifts. The beauty—both of body and soul—has arguably been the most powerful evangelical force for Christianity in history. Why? Because men crave it, look for it, and want it permanently in their lives.

Some secular women, having tried everything, are now considering that perhaps they should be nice to their husbands instead of constantly nagging and voicing their disappointment and rage to him. With 70 percent of divorces initiated by women, there is ample blame to attribute to husbands, but little to no discussion about what women might be contributing to the split.

In a shocking admonition, love expert Andrea Miller over at *Your Tango*, a website dedicated to love and relationships—which also has a section on zodiac signs and horoscopes and isn't remotely Catholic—has suggested the radical idea that a wife's job is, in fact, to make her husband happy. She explains, "Too often these women—even the strongest, smartest, most independent of them—weirdly believe

8   Bill Johnson, "A Lifestyle of Peace," *Bethel Church Podcast*, September 16, 2018, http://podcasts.ibethel.org/en/podcasts/a-lifestyle-of-peace.

that if they inflict enough pain back onto their partners or exact enough control of them, they'll suddenly get with the program. Instead, the opposite usually happens. Their partners—not feeling loved enough and tired of feeling nagged, controlled, and criticized—do the opposite. They withdraw and tune out. And the cycle of drama and dysfunction only becomes more vicious and protracted."[9]

Miller goes on to explain that after realizing the pain she was inflicting upon her spouse wasn't making either of them happy, she tried something else: tenderness, less judgment and punishment, and more affection. The results, she explains, were brilliant. "I started tuning much more actively into my husband—prioritizing him, touching him regularly (holding his hand, sitting very close to him, hugging him, rubbing his shoulders, etc), more actively praising and appreciating him, and—crucially—not letting my ego get the best of me and not letting my need to be right lead to Armageddon. As a result, I have managed to bring out the best in my husband."[10]

While bringing out the best in her husband, Miller brought out the best of herself—kind, warm, thoughtful, compassionate. For decades, women have been told that somehow, we can be happy without these things, but the real secret is as old as poetry and song.

---

[9]   Andrea Miller, "Yes, Ladies, It Is YOUR Job to Make Your Husband Happy," *Your Tango*, April 14, 2017, https://www.yourtango.com/2017301821/yes-ladies-wife-job-make-husband-happy-marriage.

[10]   Ibid.

Arriving at true beauty is one of those ironic qualities that populate ancient story telling—it arrives as soon as it is no longer sought. The truly beautiful woman knows that her real goal isn't superficial beauty. And it is the wise man who knows that this woman must exist and is worth seeking. Sadly, such women are not easy to find. As a result, men are left with surrogates that may briefly satiate the body but will never satisfy the soul.

Yes, the beauty of women will save the world far more quickly than any painting or sonata. The real battle is to remind those made to be beautiful to embrace it at its Source. It is not found in any cosmetic surgery, diets, or facial cream. Nor is it in seduction, sarcasm, cynicism, cursing, narcissism, greedy ambition, or power. It is simply in embracing the lives of others, allowing them to live in us, and then to serve their needs. It may not always be glamorous, but it is always beautiful.

In the end, the desires of women's hearts are to be beautiful, to be fruitful, to have their dignity respected, and most essentially, to be known and loved. Mary is the perfect model of how all of these things come to pass in the one who is loved by God and who has an authentic relationship with him. Living Catholicism offers women all of these. "You open your hand, you satisfy the desire of every living thing" (Ps 145:16).

Part IV

Modern Women and Mary

CHAPTER 10

Imitating Mary

"The holier a woman is, the more she is a woman."

—Leon Bloy

A look at women and girls in the Church today gives us a rather dismal picture. Teenagers, who may have had a devotion to Our Lady and Jesus when they were smaller, have quickly abandoned it for more glittery diversions, particularly the interests of their peers, funneled to them through *Teen Vogue, Seventeen,* TV sitcoms, Hollywood films, and social media. The Church—appearing outdated and boring—quickly becomes irrelevant and a nuisance in comparison to these new-found charms of life. In such a culture, Mass attendance and reception of the sacraments become boxes to be checked off for parents. Years later, perhaps when it is time to get married or a baby is on the way, the old habit of faith might creep back in. But this not-yet-prodigal daughter may only be back with her body and not with her heart. The heart for Christ she had as a young child is still cold, frozen by the cares of the world. She has a desire to get married in a beautiful church, but more for the show of it than any spiritual reason. Or perhaps she has a desire to baptize her own child, but only because it seems like the right thing to do. She goes to Mass out of obligation, but she's restless like she was as a teenager. The power of the Mass and the presence of Christ in the Eucharist scarcely penetrate her soul as her mind wanders to her to-do list, travel plans, and work projects. Whatever it is, love of a divine Savior doesn't find a way to focus her attention.

The Church has lost the majority of women. Even many women who populate the pews are not living, thinking, praying, and loving with the Church. They tolerate it for one reason or another, while feeling themselves keenly outside of it. There is no intimacy between her and the God who comes down from heaven and offers himself to her everyday; there is no stirring of love for the God who has given her everything; there is no awareness that many of the things she does in her life cause him tremendous pain. This absence of what ought to be there is the tug of the anti-Mary.

Despite all of this pressure against women and the depth of the sins against the family in particular, the specific target—women—tells us much about the age in which we are living. French priest Fr. Andre Feuillet, who experienced the painful scars of the twentieth century, wrote this in 1974: "The Christian Church is presently experiencing a very severe crisis. The most evangelical way of viewing this, without in any way trying to minimize it and without ceasing to call evil what is so in fact, is to see in this terrible trial the *painful childbearing of a new Christian world.* Just like the time of the Passion of Christ, these times we live in are very especially the *Hour of the Woman* above all, therefore, the Hour of the Woman par excellence of the new covenant, the Hour of Mary."[1]

While Fr. Feuillet was referring to the Church in the immediate aftermath of the Second Vatican Council, his remarks extend well beyond the 1970s and can be applied equally to today. We are experiencing a passion unlike any other, particularly as it is directed at women, the soil of society, which is why the solution must start with women.

Mary, Mary, and Mary

As we saw in the previous chapters, there are strong desires in the female heart. Most of what is wrong in the world today is an effort by women to meet those desires, but in misguided ways. It is only when we tap into God, into the Trinity, that these desires can be met—and not just met, but exceeded in ways beyond our comprehension.

Getting to that point happens when we follow closely in the footsteps of Our Lady. Women are all called, whether we know it or not, to imitate Mary. In Scripture, at the foot of the cross, Mary is there, along with two other women named Mary. For years, I had just found this confusing, "Couldn't the Evangelists have used different names?" Finally, in a moment of clarity, it occurred to me that they are all named Mary for a real reason: our salvation comes at the foot of the cross when we are present to Christ like Mary was. All women are called to be like her at the foot of the cross, to be

---

[1]   Feuillet, 239.

present to him. Out of this great mystery flows the "blood and water" that brings real fruitfulness to our lives.

Rediscovering Mary's Virtues

While it is easy to suggest that women should just "be like Mary," working out the practical bits of how to do this is vitally important, particularly when we lack good role models to show us the way to do it. One of the biggest obstacles to imitating Mary is that, in order to be like her, we have to understand her virtues. As we saw in chapter 7, Mary's virtues aren't always easily accessible for contemporary women. It shouldn't surprise us, then, when women say, "I just don't feel a connection with Mary." I have heard this over and over again from women. "Yes, I understand," is always my response. For years and years, this is exactly how I felt. In my mind, I could clearly comprehend why Mary was important, and I had a deep fascination with places like Lourdes and Fatima. But in my heart, all my emotions felt cold and unengaged. And it wasn't because I had an unloving mother; I have a wonderful mother. There was something more to it that I could never put my finger on.

Despite the coldness of my emotions, I always knew on an intellectual level that Mary was close. I kept her at the fore of my mind, consecrating myself to her and praying the Rosary daily: during long drives, long runs, or before sleep at night. But no matter how much I prayed, there was always that missing piece.

I prayed for a long time about this, wishing to have that emotional spark or connection. Eventually, I resigned myself to thinking that perhaps when I became a mother, once I experienced what it was like to have my own child, I would feel and "know her from the inside." So I waited. And waited. Finally, at a few weeks shy of my thirty-sixth birthday, I had my first child. And, yes, suddenly, I understood what it was like to give until you could give no more, to love with a ferocious love, and to want to suffer everything with your child just to help him or her carry burdens. *I finally understood how Mary must love us.*

One of the things I didn't realize, however, was that my quest to understand Our Lady started even before I was married with children. It came to my attention that most of the things promoted by women in our culture—being outspoken, assertive, independent, and ambitious—weren't producing the kind of happiness I expected. I started paying attention to music, poetry, and movies, anywhere I could find evidence of what made for truly timeless and great women, not just those propped up by our culture.

And what did I find? Remarkable and beautiful portrayals of women using interior capacities I had never thought about before: kindness, compassion, listening, anticipating the needs of others, sincerity, and goodness. Getting married and having children only made me go deeper to find and live these newly discovered virtues. I marveled at the fruits—my friends got closer; my children grew contented; my husband became more loving—all because I turned from self-absorption to looking to the needs of others. Living these virtues was the missing piece of the puzzle I couldn't see. I needed to live Mary's virtues to understand her from the inside. We see them in Scripture: silence, obedience, kindness, meekness, and tenderness. I couldn't find comfort in Our Lady before this realization because her virtues were foreign to me. Our comfort generally resides in the familiar, and Marian values simply aren't that for most of us. It might take some time, lots of prayer, and plenty of time in silence, but these virtues don't have to remain foreign to us.

Rely Upon Your Mother

Another struggle many people face is the reality that we can't see Mary, so how do we know that she is with us? This is where faith comes in to play. Most of us have an ideal of what a good mother is and what a good mother does. Mary is the perfect mother, tending to all the details of our lives, so long as we are open to letting that relationship grow and we are open to her. Many a saint has attested to her maternal intercession, her protection, her help, that has never been known to fail. Even the demons speak of her attentiveness to humanity, like these words recorded during an exorcism:

> She is full of light. She blinds me, blinds me, cursed! When she was born, the world stopped for a moment. All creation stopped to look at her, all creation: the stars, the air, the fire, the water, the ground. All creation stopped. No one noticed besides me. I knew it. I knew who she was, and I could not do anything. I could not touch her. She was pure, pure. Enough, enough. Do not make me remember! She is like balsam. She soothes wounds, those that are the deepest. If you only knew how much she loves you, you would live your lives joyfully, without fear, without sin.

Through her, you would understand how much hurt
sin causes the Son.[2]

Another demon is reported to have said, "She is on a
cloud and is saying, 'Be calm, I am here with you, and I
am helping you.'"[3] There is a reason why so many of her
beautiful titles are about her assistance: Our Lady Help of
Christians, Star of the Sea, Mother of Mercy, Mother of the
Church, Mother of Charity. She is not a helicopter mother,
only buzzing in to move us on from one task to the next, but
a true mother who is always with us.

We are invited to have an actual relationship with Our
Lady, not just to rotely say our prayers without seeing her
engaging in our lives in a real, tangible way. Certainly, we
won't know what she is doing behind the scenes, but we can
draw nearer to her through the Mass and the sacraments, as
well as through the Rosary and through Marian consecration. Padre Pio (St. Pio) has called the Rosary "the weapon"
for our times. Over and over again, in Marian apparitions,
Our Lady has asked for the faithful to pray the Rosary. Even
the demons are keenly aware of its power:

> If you all knew it, I would be destroyed in less than
> a second. If you all said the rosary, this bastard thing
> here, with faith! Do you know what she does when
> you say this chain? She takes your hand. She extends
> it towards heaven and takes the hand of your God.
> And through this prayer, this chain of (swear words

2   Bamonte, *Virgin Mary and Exorcism*, 87–88.
3   Ibid., 69.

follow), she approximates the two hands and brings them together so they touch. When these two hands meet, she exults, exults, exults, and gets on her knees and prays. Only a few men touch that hand because many times they take their hand away from hers because they do not want to do it. They do not want to do it thanks to me who am their god. But those who succeed, but those who succeed, they are fully aware of it and she exults. You see that she kneels down and kisses the pierced feet of the Son.[4]

The fruitfulness of the Rosary is hard to exaggerate, especially when looking at the history of the Church and the many ways in which Our Lady has helped those who have prayed it devotedly. Blessed Alan de la Roche had a vision of Mary in which she told him about how the world looks when the Rosary is prayed devotedly by the multitudes:

Through the rosary, hardened sinners of both sexes became converted and started to lead a holy life, bemoaning their past sins with genuine tears of contrition. Even children performed unbelievable penances: devotion to my Son and to me spread so thoroughly that it almost seemed as though angels were living on earth. The Faith was gaining, and many Catholics longed to shed their blood for it and fight against the heretics. Thus, through the sermons of my very dear Dominic and through the power of the rosary, the heretics' lands were all brought under the Church.

---

[4]   Ibid., 111.

People used to give munificent alms; hospitals and churches were built. People led moral and law-abiding lives and worked wonders for the glory of God. Holiness and unworldliness flourished; the clergy were exemplary, princes were just, people lived at peace with each other and justice and equity reigned in the guilds and in the homes.

I must not fail to mention the signs and wonders that I have wrought in different lands through the holy rosary: I have stopped pestilences and put an end to horrible wars as well as to bloody crimes, and through the rosary people have found the courage to flee temptation.[5]

The beads of the rosary, like the tiny stones used by David to vanquish Goliath, have much more power than we might ever know.

Be a Daughter to the Mother

For as much discussion as there is about Our Lady being our mother, we must also be daughters to her, open to being taught and directed by her maternal care. Von Le Fort says, "Mary stands for her daughters, but her daughters must also stand for her."[6] St. Faustina, who had many engagements with both Christ and his Mother, wrote down the words of Mary in her dairy: "Before Holy Communion I saw the Blessed

---

[5]   As quoted in St. Louis de Montfort, *The Secret of the Rosary*, 119. Our Lady's Word to Blessed Alan de la Roche (Calloway, Appendix B)

[6]   von le Fort, *Eternal Woman*, 108.

Mother inconceivably beautiful. Smiling at me, She said to me, *My daughter, at God's command I am to be, in a special and exclusive way your Mother; but I desire that you, too, in a special way, be My child.*[7] Mary told her daughter about the three virtues she wanted her to practice that are most pleasing to her and to God: "*The first is humility, humility, and once again humility; the second virtue, purity; the third virtue, love of God. As My daughter, you must especially radiate with these virtues.*" St. Faustina continues, "When the conversation ended, She pressed me to Her Heart and disappeared. When I regained the use of my senses, my heart became so wonderfully attracted to these virtues; and I practice them faithfully. They are as though engraved in my heart."[8]

Mary's ways may seem foreign to us, but through a real relationship, she will help us to imitate and follow her and her Son more closely.

Not a Victim

Despite living in an age of victimhood, I've never come across a book recognizing the victim status of Our Lady. It is a curious thing to consider that here is a woman, the Mother of God, no less, who watched her Son be unjustly tortured and killed in the most barbarous of circumstances because of our sins, and yet nary a feminist has honored her special place as a victim.

---

[7]   Maria Faustina Kowalska, *Diary: Divine Mercy in my Soul* (Marian Press, 2005), 1414–15.

[8]   Ibid.

I realize it's ridiculous to expect this since feminists rarely warm up to Our Lady. (Why just go with "the woman" when you can worship a goddess?) But what it should remind us of is that this is a woman whose Son died for our sins. If she were not perfect, if she were stained with sin, or was open to the devil's tempting, she would be the one pointing her finger at all of us. The rage and anger of a mother in this situation would be entirely justified.

What is truly miraculous, and what tells us she is better than we could ever imagine, is that rather than expressing justifiable rage toward us, she comes to us, the guilty, as a tender mother offering her love, protection, wisdom, and guidance. She knows well what the crucifixion cost her Son. She doesn't want his bloody sacrifice to be in vain. What she wants is mercy, love, sacrifice, prayer, and to bring each of us closer to him. This is how she guides us. Not in the path of rage, anger, vengeance, and victimhood. The reality that she has not only forgiven us but loves us as her own children is a great reminder that she is a wonderful gift and the intense model of mercy that we are to follow.

CHAPTER II

Six Ways to Combat the Anti-Mary

"Pray, trust, and don't worry."

—St. Pio of Pietrelcina

Beyond imitating Mary, there is more that can be done to rebuild our culture and combat the anti-Mary, the culture of people "who call evil good and good evil, who put darkness for light and light for darkness, who put bitter for sweet and sweet for bitter!" (Is 5:20). People sometimes suggest that we should just return to the 1950s for the answer to our struggles, but if the 1950s had been so idyllic, the 1960s would never have happened; as we saw before, there were already deep wounds within the faith and society as a whole that opened the door to the anti-Marian culture. So, while returning to that time (as if that were even possible) might bring back some of the innocence and integrity we once had, it won't solve all our problems. Instead of trying to turn back the clock, here are six specific ways we can combat the anti-Marian culture moving forward.

1. Become a Spiritual Adult

In 1906, a sociologist pointed out that a civilization can't regenerate itself without spiritual adulthood. Without parents who pass on to their children the keys to spiritual maturity, a civilization simply cannot thrive or survive. Part of the current popular appeal of Jordan Peterson, particularly for men, is that he tells them to grow up, to do things that adults have always done in the past, instead of coddling them and allowing them to remain adolescents for the rest of their lives.

There are generations of people who don't know what it means to even be an adult, much less a spiritual adult. Spiritual adulthood usually depends on a basic level of maturity. One priest who forms seminarians confided to me that the first thing he has to teach many of them is how to be adults. Basic attitudes and habits like taking responsibility for one's actions, being considerate of others, using good manners, and punctuality are taught first. Grace builds upon nature, so there must be a functioning adult before there can be spiritual adulthood.

There are, of course, plenty of examples among the saints of children who showed remarkable spiritual maturity, such as St. Maria Goretti and Fatima seer St. Jacinta Marto. These children certainly would not have needed "adult schooling." Jacinta, at her tender age of nine, was already well equipped to live in the adult world, having worked long hours as a shepherdess. And Maria took over running her household at nine after her father died and her mother had to work in the fields to support the family. The classroom of struggle and suffering go a long way in transforming a child into a grown-up.

The on-ramp to spiritual maturity isn't easily found in the old familiar places—from the pulpit, Catholic schools, or in our homes. Our penchant for avoiding pain and suffering at any cost hasn't helped. Part of being an adult is to stop complaining, whining, and blaming others for what is wrong and seek out real solutions.

The problem of spiritual immaturity will only be solved through our own prayer, sacrifice, service, selflessness, and seeking—through our own concerted effort to grow into spiritual adulthood. Part of that process means passing it on to others, particularly our children, but we can only give what we have. There is a reason airlines suggest putting your own oxygen mask on first before assisting your child, and the same applies in the realm of the spiritual. You aren't much use unconscious.

The biggest irony, of course, is that the responsible adult finds the key to spiritual maturity in childlike trust. Like the Magi following that star, even with all their pomp, intellectual acumen, and riches, they too had to become like trusting children by following a star. In their humility, they were led to find the Christ Child.

2. Strive for a Holy Family

The first thing we have to recognize is the damage that has been done to the family. Jennifer Roback Morse says, "The women's liberation movement, in particular, gave us more things to quarrel about, more grievances and grudges, more permission to focus on ourselves, and easier exit options. What we really needed was more love, all of us. More love from parent to child, from child to parent, and above all, between husbands and wives."[1] Our problem is not over-nurturing but under-nurturing our relationships. Reclaiming meals together, more time away from screens, and listening to each other can go a long way. Remember that Satan likes division, disunity, and confusion. Combatting these at home is critical.

We also need parents to see that they have a common mission to sanctify each other and their children. It isn't just the mom's job, or the school's job, but it is the job of both parents first and foremost. This was one of the troubles with the 1950s: faith became more threadbare and women were left at home without the spiritual sustenance they needed. Rather than doubling down and saying, "I need my husband and I to grow closer spiritually to raise up a holy family," they ended up opting for the easier option: to just leave home and do what their husbands were doing.

Without a common mission, a great division can happen between husband and wife. "The husband can grow to see his family as a burden getting in the way of his higher purpose which is his career," Noelle Mering explains. Meanwhile, "the mother's mission is trivialized. She begins to sense her own work at home is not their common life's work but merely her burden to endure in service of a higher mission that is his alone and for which she has not acquiesced."[2]

---

[1]   Morse, *Sexual State*, 203.

[2]   Noelle Mering, "How Theology of Home Makes Men Heroic," *Helena Daily*, October 1, 2018, https://www.helenadaily.com/

When there is no unity of purpose, Mering continues, "these duties seem merely menial and heavy—and merely menial and heavy work will quickly feel suffocating and oppressive for whomever shoulders it. Resentment calcifies like a tumor as husband and wife become competitors rather than allies." [3]Beyond a common purpose, there are other ways to sanctify your home, such as having your home blessed, and using sacramentals regularly, like holy water and blessed salt. Decorating with icons or religious art serves as a reminder of our final purpose, while offering the quiet support of the saints and Our Lady. Hospitality, hosting others and creating community through good meals and great conversation, is also an important way to build up your own family and bring community together.

3. Go Deeper into Motherhood and Spiritual Motherhood

Our culture will only be able to renew itself if we reclaim both physical motherhood and spiritual motherhood. Jennifer Roback Morse wisely reminds us, "We all need someone who personally, unconditionally cares about us."[4] Not one of us can be the perfect parent, but this is why we have grace, the sacraments, and the wisdom of the Holy Spirit to help us parent the children God has given us.

St. Angela Merici speaks about the importance of a consecrated woman's love for her spiritual children. She writes,

---

theologyofhome/2018/10/1/toh-men-temporary-title.
3   Ibid.
4   Roback Morse, *Sexual State*, 255.

"Bear them . . . engraved upon your heart—not merely their names, but their conditions and states, whatever they may be. This will not be difficult for you if you embrace them with a living love."

Healing is also an important part of spiritual motherhood. With so many broken people around us, being aware of resources like Project Rachel and other post-abortive ministries is important, as are other outreach groups, like Catholic Charities and solid recourses for psychological help. Our gifts of listening, asking questions, and just being present to others can go a long way—further than many of us believe possible.

4. Fill Up Your Spiritual Tank

As women, we have all felt it: that desire just to go shopping and distract ourselves from our daily struggles, to delight in something new in our wardrobe or some other bobble to distract us. These kinds of distractions are exactly that, distractions keeping us from looking into the real piece that is missing: our longing for God.

The key to keep us on track is always to be mindful that these distractions are signs of something deeper and that we must nourish our prayer lives, nourish the soul, with real food. We must come to understand how much we are treasured daughters of God the Father and that his provision extends to us in every waking and sleeping moment of our lives. When we know that "all things work for good for those who love God" (Rom 8:28) and reject the lie that we are orphans, then envy, greed, fear, and boredom have no hold on our lives. A spirit of gratitude for this relationship with our Maker and for all the many gifts in our lives, no matter how small, can also dissipate envy's venom, or the restless spirit that can overtake us.

We must make prayer an essential part of our daily lives, finding God whenever we can. There will be obstacles, particularly depending on what season of life one is in, but silence and prayer must become a priority.

5. Be Aware of Satan's Entry Points

As we have seen in previous chapters, our culture is saturated with the occult, in large ways and small. It's hard to escape it, but escape it we must if we are going to get ourselves and our families to heaven. Vigilance with the culture has to be constant because Satan will creep in wherever he can.

Avoiding certain obvious places is good, like astrology, tarot card readings, fortune tellers, the enneagram, goddess material, the *Sante Muerte* cult, and yoga. Satan likes to hide his evil among the sugar, so constant vigilance is important. Also, be on guard about what your children are watching; keep an eye on their screen time and social media accounts. Porn introduction and sexting requests can begin between the ages of eight and nine and get worse as children get older.

Also, being aware of the areas of malcontent in your life is crucial because Satan will use these negative emotions to entrap you. Actively listening for dark lies about yourself, or comparing yourself to others, is a good place to look for his foothold. Rejecting his lies while embracing charity, compassion, humility, and acceptance are great ways to free yourself from his bondage. Like St. Paul reminded the Ephesians, who were under the spell of Artemis:

> Therefore, putting away falsehood, speak the truth, each one to his neighbor, for we are members one of another. Be angry but do not sin; do not let the sun set on your anger, and do not leave room for the devil. The thief must no longer steal, but rather labor, doing honest work with his [own] hands, so that he may have something to share with one in need. No foul language should come out of your mouths, but only such as is good for needed edification, that it may impart grace to those who hear. And do not grieve the holy Spirit of God, with which you were sealed for the day of redemption. All bitterness, fury, anger, shouting, and reviling must be removed from you, along with all malice. [And] be kind to one another, compassionate, forgiving one another as God has forgiven you in Christ. (Eph 4:25–32 NABRE)

6. Kindness and Tenderness

I asked a dear friend of mine, while she was slowly dying from the ravages of cancer, if there was anything in her life that she wished she could change. As a Catholic, I knew she had been to confession regularly and squared away many of the regrets of her life. But the one thing she mentioned that stuck with me was that she wished she had been more kind to others throughout her life. It seemed a rather insignificant thing to me at the time, but ten years later, it has sunk in.

There is a beautiful book by Fr. Lawrence G. Lovasik, best known for his children's books about the faith, entitled *The Hidden Power of Kindness: A Practical Handbook for Souls Who Dare to Transform the World One Deed at a Time.*[5] Kindness is another one of the gifts hidden in plain sight that we often miss; in fact, it's one of God's greatest gifts. Fr. Lovasik writes, "The least kind action is greater than the greatest wrong. The smallest kindness can lift a heavy weight."[6] He explains further that "a single act of kindness throws out roots in all directions, and the roots spring up and make new trees. The greatest work that kindness does to others is that it makes them kind themselves. . . . As you become kinder yourself by practicing kindness, so the people you are kind to, if they were kind before, learn to be kinder, or if they were not kind before, learn how to be kind."[7] We all know the burden that comes when someone holds us in contempt, but kindness can lighten that load. "Kindness drives gloom and darkness from souls and puts hope into fainting hearts. It sweetens sorrow and lessens pain. It discovers unsuspected beauty of human character and calls forth a response from all that is best in souls. Kindness purifies, glorifies, and ennobles all that it touches."[8]

We have forgotten the power of kindness as a culture and even within our faith. But here again, Our Lady models

---

5   Lawrence G. Lovasik, *The Hidden Power of Kindness: A Practical Handbook for Souls Who Dare to Transform the World One Deed at a Time* (Sophia Institute Press, 1999).

6   Ibid., 10.

7   Ibid., 11.

8   Ibid.

perfect kindness that comes with perfect love. She is never rude or belittling, always open to trying to bring the stray sheep home instead of offering them contempt. Catholics can sometimes be justly accused of being callus or angry. Certainly, there is much to be angry about in our world today, but contempt, rage, and belittling those we are called to love is not the response that will bring healing to our culture.

CHAPTER 12

Helping the Walking Wounded

"I therefore . . . beg you to lead a life worthy of the calling
to which you have been called, with all lowliness and
meekness, with patience, forbearing one another in love."

—Ephesians 4:1–2

For the past five decades, the painful irony is that women, not men, have been their own worst enemy. Feminism was supposed to improve women's lives. Unfortunately, feminist responses to the world's problems have actually further enslaved women in poverty, broken relationships, diseased bodies, empty homes, and so on. Sadly, this new bondage in which women find themselves, rather than being rightly blamed on feminism, has also been turned into a cause célèbre of the movement and a rallying cry to continuing fighting. And so women bind themselves even more tightly in their chains.

Like every good fairy tale, in the end, we know that authentic beauty, goodness, truth, and honesty can only be hidden, abused, and despised for so long. One day, the flash and fancy of feminist ideology will finally be revealed for what it is and it will no longer be judged the fairest of them all. But this will not happen without a lot of prayer, fasting, and interceding for the women who have come under the anti-Marian spell.

St. Ignatius of Loyola, a master of spiritual direction, drew out for all Christians to see the pronounced interior difference between the soul living in a state of grace and one who is not. The soul who is seeking God is motivated by interior joys, consolations, and encouragements, while the one moving away from God skips from mortal sin to mortal sin. Despite the built-in struggles that come from living in mortal sin (e.g., difficult relationships, self-defeating activities), a turnaround generally doesn't happen until one hits rock bottom and realizes something has to change. Only then, like the prodigal son (or daughter), are eyes raised to God. And fortunately, Mary will be there to help.

As the Mother of Mercy, Mary spoke directly to St. Bridget about what her mercy means in practical terms. "I am the Queen of heaven and the Mother of Mercy. I am the joy of the just and the door through which sinners come to God." She continued, "There are no sinners on earth so unfortunate as to be beyond my mercy. For even if they receive nothing else through my intercession, at least they receive the grace of being less tempted by the devils than they would otherwise be." Even after death, Our Lady explained, "unless the last irrevocable sentence (of damnation) has been pronounced against them, there are no persons so abandoned by God that they will not return to Him and find mercy, if they invoke my aid."[1]

Walking With the Wounded

The widespread prevalence of abortion, contraception, lesbianism, and the rest have led us to a place where we are surrounded by the walking wounded. We know that Christ does not want these women left abandoned, but embraced, tended to, and cared for. Doling out this charity is no simple task when they are living with sinful and prideful blindness, and yet, we must not abandon them.

Every now and again, a film will come to the big screen that embodies an important idea for a culture. The Disney film *Moana* offers an unexpected modern-day parable to help us love women who have been caught in the cultural snares.

The film is about a teenager, Moana, next in line to become chief of her tribe. She is tasked by the sea to hunt down the demigod Maui to save her island and her tribe from death emanating from the goddess of life, Te Fiti. Millennia ago, Maui stole the heart from Te Fiti, and without it, Te Fiti no longer has the capacity to give life, leaving the oceans, fish, island vegetation, and humanity to slowly die. The ocean brought Te Fiti's heart to Moana so that she and Maui could return it to where it belongs. In short, Moana must save her people.

---

[1]   Reprinted in St. Alphonsus Ligouri, *The Glories of Mary* (Ligouri, 2000), 23.

The largest obstacle to Maui and Moana's mission is Te Ka, a fiery lava monster that they must conquer to reach their final goal. Even Maui is reluctant to battle Te Ka, having been beaten by it in the past. Maui engages the fiery figure, but in the battle, Te Ka is able to fracture Maui's hook, the source of his demigod power. Knowing that one more crack would ruin his powers, Maui leaves Moana alone to fight the massive angry beast.

Moana bravely works out her strategy to avoid the fire balls, flaming fingers, and angry wrath of Te Ka. Deftly maneuvering her outrigger, Moana sails to find the vulnerable spots where she can make her way past the monster's craggy and barren island. She finally gets through, but with Te Ka on her heels. Just when it looks as if there is no escape from Te Ka's reach, Maui returns, saving Moana. Moana scrambles up the craggy island to her destination where she can finally return Te Fiti's heart. At the highest point—not knowing where to place the heart—she looks down in the water and sees the silhouette of a woman's body, but the woman isn't there. She looks back to the raging Te Ka and sees in the chest of the fiery beast the same symbol that is on the heart stone in her hand. It is then that Moana realizes that Te Ka is really Te Fiti—the fiery beast is really the heartless goddess of life. She must give the heart stone back to Te Ka.

As she approaches the thrashing beast, Moana says, "This is not who you are." She holds out the heart stone for the monster to see, and suddenly, it is subdued and focused. The monster lowers itself down to look at Moana and the tiny stone in her hand. And then the beast—gentle and sad—allows the heart to be returned to its rightful place. It is only then that the angry, lava-filled beast is transformed into a green, fertile, gentle, and beautiful goddess.

While this is a Disney story drawing heavily from Polynesian mythology, it is an archetype or guide to understanding what happens to a woman when her true heart is removed. The results are dramatic, devastating, and widespread. And yet the antidote is very simple: to remind her that "this is not who you are." The world of the anti-Mary is not who we are, not what we are made for. It would be wonderful if the solution were as simple as showing women entranced by the anti-Mary a vision of their own heart, but it is not. We have to remind women that radical feminism isn't who they really are. Striving to be like men isn't who they really are. Being consumed by rage, anxiety, and malice isn't who they really are. And living as if there is no God isn't who they really are. As we engage them, it would be good to remember that our battle, as St. Paul reminded the Ephesians and us, isn't really with them but with the devil: "For our struggle is not with flesh and blood but with the principalities, with the powers, with the world rulers of this present darkness, with the evil spirits in the heavens" (Eph 6:12 NABRE).

We must be the women and men who courageously go outside of our comfort zones, who are willing to tackle monsters bigger than we are. We, like Moana and Maui, are tasked with giving women their hearts back. Compelled by lies, savvy marketing, and dark influences, women have traded it away for things that will never satisfy, that will never give true life, that will never gain them what they yearn for in the deepest layers of their soul. We must restore the heart or our future, like the islands in the myth, will remain barren, dying a slow death.

As ever, Catholicism is the only antidote left standing to deal with all of these struggles in the feminine heart. Ours is not a trendy diversion, as women from the last twenty centuries can attest, but the most powerful force on Earth when unleashed. Even this lengthy list of obstacles to our faith is nothing compared to the transforming power of God. We can debate all we want about what will appeal to women and try to contort the Church and its message into many things, but the real appeal is what it has always been: Christ. He offers the kind of love that women's hearts crave—to be known just as we are, intimately, uniquely, and purposefully. It was this love that transformed Magdalene. It is this love that brought us Sts. Helen, Hildegard, Joan of Arc, Bridget, Bernadette, and all the Catherines (Alexandria, Siena, Labouré), to name a few. And it is this same love that can transform the hearts of every woman.

But this kind of love is not currently available in the public square, and that's where the real work is for Christians. We cannot leave it to someone else to tell women where they can find true happiness, even if they don't yet have the ears to hear us. Somewhere, seeds of our example, our prayers, and the truth will sink in—if only because it is different from what everyone else says. And when it does, then the soul will be ready to face the God-Man, who fulfills the desire of every living thing.

Important Prayers to Combat the Anti-Mary

Marian Prayers

Hail Mary

Hail Mary,
Full of Grace,
The Lord is with thee.
Blessed art thou among women,
and blessed is the fruit
of thy womb, Jesus.
Holy Mary,
Mother of God,
pray for us sinners now,
and at the hour of our death. Amen.

Memorare

The Memorare prayer was a favorite of St. Teresa of Calcutta. She would say a "flying novena" when she had an intention that needed to be answered quickly. Eight Memorares for the intention and one more in thanksgiving.

Remember, O most gracious Virgin Mary, that never was it known that anyone who fled to thy protection, implored thy help, or sought thine intercession was left unaided.

Inspired by this confidence, I fly unto thee, O Virgin of virgins, my mother; to thee do I come, before thee I stand, sinful and sorrowful. O Mother of the Word Incarnate, despise not my petitions, but in thy mercy hear and answer me. Amen.

Prayers of Other Saints

Prayer to Defeat the Devil by St. Anna Maria Taigi

The Incorrupt Patroness of Mothers and Families, St. Anna Maria Taigi

Prostrate at thy feet, O Great Queen of Heaven, we venerate thee with the deepest reverence and we confess that thou art the Daughter of the Father, the Mother of the Divine Word, the Spouse of the Holy Ghost. Thou art the storekeeper and the almoner of the Divine Mercies. For this reason, we call thee Mother of Divine Compassion.

Behold us here in affliction and anguish. Deign to show us thy true love. We beg thee to ask the Holy Trinity most fervently to grant us the grace ever to conquer the devil, and the world and our evil passions; the efficacious grace that sanctifies the just, converts sinners, destroys heresies, enlightens infidels and brings all men to the true faith.

Obtain for us this great gift that all the world may form but one people united in the One True Church.

Mary, Mother of Holy Hope, pray for us.[2]

---

[2]   Larry Peterson, "A Laywoman's Prayer to Our Lady for the grace

St. Patrick's Lorica

I arise today
Through a mighty strength, the invocation of the Trinity,
Through a belief in the Threeness,
Through confession of the Oneness
Of the Creator of creation.

I arise today
Through the strength of Christ's birth and His baptism,
Through the strength of His crucifixion and His burial,
Through the strength of His resurrection and His ascension,
Through the strength of His descent for the judgment of doom.

I arise today
Through the strength of the love of cherubim,
In obedience of angels,
In service of archangels,
In the hope of resurrection to meet with reward,
In the prayers of patriarchs,
In preachings of the apostles,
In faiths of confessors,
In innocence of virgins,
In deeds of righteous men.

I arise today
Through the strength of heaven;

to Conquer the Devil," *Aleteia*, August 22, 2018, https://aleteia.org/2018/08/22/a-laywomans-prayer-to-our-lady-for-the-grace-to-conquer-the-devil/.

Light of the sun,
Splendor of fire,
Speed of lightning,
Swiftness of the wind,
Depth of the sea,
Stability of the earth,
Firmness of the rock.
I arise today
Through God's strength to pilot me;
God's might to uphold me,
God's wisdom to guide me,
God's eye to look before me,
God's ear to hear me,
God's word to speak for me,
God's hand to guard me,
God's way to lie before me,
God's shield to protect me,
God's hosts to save me
From snares of the devil,
From temptations of vices,
From every one who desires me ill,
Afar and anear,
Alone or in a multitude.
I summon today all these powers between me and evil,
Against every cruel merciless power that opposes my body
and soul,
Against incantations of false prophets,
Against black laws of pagandom,
Against false laws of heretics,
Against craft of idolatry,

Against spells of women and smiths and wizards,
Against every knowledge that corrupts man's body and soul.
Christ shield me today
Against poison, against burning,
Against drowning, against wounding,
So that reward may come to me in abundance.

Christ with me, Christ before me, Christ behind me,
Christ in me, Christ beneath me, Christ above me,
Christ on my right, Christ on my left,
Christ when I lie down, Christ when I sit down,
Christ in the heart of every man who thinks of me,
Christ in the mouth of every man who speaks of me,
Christ in the eye that sees me,
Christ in the ear that hears me.

I arise today
Through a mighty strength, the invocation of the Trinity,
Through a belief in the Threeness,
Through a confession of the Oneness
Of the Creator of creation.

St. Patrick (ca. 377)

St. Michael Prayer

This prayer originated from Pope Leo XIII after he was given a devastating vision of the future. He asked that it be prayed after every Mass to defeat the devil and all of his efforts to corrupt the world.

St. Michael the Archangel,
defend us in battle.

Be our defense against the wickedness and snares of the devil.
May God rebuke him, we humbly pray,
and do thou,
O Prince of the heavenly hosts,
by the power of God,
thrust into hell Satan,
and all the evil spirits,
who prowl about the world
seeking the ruin of souls. Amen.

ACKNOWLEDGMENTS

"Most writers," Gloria Steinem once wrote, "don't like writing, they like having written."[1] This might be the only thing she said that I can agree with. Book writing is never a project done in isolation, but involves the encouragement, love, and input from so many which makes it tolerable and sometimes even enjoyable. This book was vastly improved by the input and experiences of Sue Ellen Browder, Leah Darrow, and Sandra Miesel. In 1969, Mallory Millett helped her sister Kate come up with the name *Sexual Politics* for her book that brought so much damage to the world. Fifty years later, she helped me name this book. This book, for so many reasons, owes a lot to Mallory's faith, courage, pluck, and wisdom.

I'm also grateful for the encouragement from Msgr. Arthur B. Calkins, Fr. Donald Calloway, David Clayton, Scott Hahn, and Mark Miravalle for this project. And I'm indebted to Fr. Peter Fegan, Fr. Jeffrey Kirby, Fr. Michael Kelly, and Fr. Stefan Starzynski for the invaluable spiritual

---

1   Joan LaLiberte, "Pocatellan captures flavor of Stanley Basin's history," *Idaho State Journal*, Page C-8, Column 3, November 19, 1976, https://quoteinvestigator.com/2014/10/18/on-writing/.

support and guidance and for the prayers of the Boldy children. The continued friendship, listening ears, and insights from Marilisa Carney, Becky Carter, Noelle Mering, Peggy Nicely, and Megan Schrieber also helped me tremendously to see this book to the finish.

I continue to be so grateful to the fine folks at TAN Books for their professionalism, vision, support, promotion, and trust in my work, particularly Brian Kennelly, Chris Cona, Christian Tappe, Robert and Conor Gallagher, Nick Vari, Caroline Green, Mara Persic, Paul Grabowski, and Katie DeMoss.

Special thanks to Kevin Knight at *The National Catholic Register* and *New Advent*, Carl Olson at *Catholic World Report*, Joy Pullman at *The Federalist*, and Robert Royal at *The Catholic Thing* for publishing several of my pieces that partially made their way into this book.

This book would never have come about without the patience, love, and sacrifices of my children and husband, Joseph. They are the ones that truly bear the brunt of the long hours required for book writing.

And finally, special thanks to my sisters, Mary, Jill, Michelle, and Danielle, to whom this book is dedicated. I marvel at their unconditional love and remain forever grateful for their gift of true sisterhood.

Excerpts from this book previously appeared in:

Catholic World Report

The Fashion of Abortion, Oct. 2, 2015

Fatima, Ideology, and the Vatican's Homosexual Crisis,
Sept. 7, 2018

The Catholic Thing

A Theology of Home, Sept. 22, 2018

The Federalist

How Acting Like a Feminist Can Ruin Your Marriage, July
28, 2017

The Patriarchy Has Been Replaced by a Stifling Matriarchy,
Sept. 7, 2017

National Catholic Register

If There Is an Antichrist, What about an Antimary?, June
1, 2017

Beware of the Poisoned Apple of Feminist Ideology, Dec.
17, 2017

Are We Witnessing the Battle Between an Antimary and an
Antichrist?, Jan. 27, 2017

The Beauty of Women Will Save the World, March 23,
2017.

While Millennials look to Adulting, We Can't forget Spiritual Adulthood, Dec. 20, 2016

Women Don't Need to Look Far to Know God's Will,
Sept. 8, 2017

Why the Women You Love Have Left the Faith, Nov. 17,
2017

A Powerful Evangelical Force Is Right Under Our Noses,
May 3, 2018